LEVEL FOUR

Sound Advice
Theory and Ear Training

Brenda Braaten and **Crystal Wiksyk**

Series Editor
Laura Beauchamp-Williamson

Illustrations by Paul McCusker

© Copyright 2006 The Frederick Harris Music Co., Limited
All Rights Reserved

ISBN 1-55440-034-1

Design & Production: First Image
Music Typesetter: Ken Gee

Library and Archives Canada Cataloguing in Publication

Braaten, Brenda, 1952-
Sound advice : theory and ear training / Brenda Braaten and
Crystal Wiksyk ; illustrations by Paul McCusker.

Accompanied by audio tracks, available online.
To be complete in 8 vol.
Complete contents: Level 1 – Level 2 – Level 3 – Level 4 –
   Level 5 – Level 6 – Level 7 – Level 8.
ISBN 1-55440-031-7 (v. 1).–ISBN 1-55440-032-5 (v. 2).–
ISBN 1-55440-033-3 (v. 3).–ISBN 1-55440-034-1 (v. 4).–
ISBN 1-55440-035-X (v. 5).–ISBN 1-55440-036-8 (v. 6).–
ISBN 1-55440-037-6 (v. 7).–ISBN 1-55440-038-4 (v. 8)

1. Music theory. 2. Ear training. I. Wiksyk, Crystal, 1959-
II. McCusker, Paul   III. Title.

MT7.B794S72 2006   781   C2005-907128-1

Contents

Preface for Teachers 6

How to Use this Book 7
Lesson Organization
Completing the Ear-Training Worksheets
Charts and Games
Suggestions for Daily Ear-Training Practice

Lesson 1

Learning Guide 10
Review of Note Values and Rests
Note-Value Comparison Chart
Ties and Dots
Beaming Notes to Show the Beat
Rhythmic Reading
One-Minute Rhythm Jumble
Theory Worksheet 14
Ear-Training Worksheet 16

Lesson 2

Learning Guide 18
Half Steps and Whole Steps
Accidentals
Enharmonic Equivalents
Major Scale Review: C, G, D, F, and B♭ Major
Scale Degree Numbers
Theory Worksheet 21
Ear-Training Worksheet 22

Lesson 3

Learning Guide 23
Key Signatures
Key Signature Shortcuts
Mad Music Game: Major Key Signatures
Theory Worksheet 25
Ear-Training Worksheet 26

Lesson 4

Learning Guide 27
Meter and Time Signatures
Adding Time Signatures and Bar Lines
Rhythmic Dictation
Theory Worksheet 29
Ear-Training Worksheet 30

Lesson 5

Learning Guide 32
Naming Major and Perfect Intervals
The Sound of Ascending Intervals
The Ascending Perfect 4th (P4)
The Ascending Major 6th (maj 6)
Theory Worksheet 34
Ear-Training Worksheet 35

Lesson 6

Learning Guide 36
Naming Minor Intervals
The Sound of Ascending Minor 2nds and 3rds
A Closer Look at Ascending Minor 2nds and 3rds
Theory Worksheet 38
Ear-Training Worksheet 39

Lesson 7

Learning Guide 40
Incomplete Measures
Review of Scale Degree Names
Phrases and Cadences
Imitation
Composing and Improvising
Theory Worksheet 42
Ear-Training Worksheet 44

Lesson 8

Learning Guide 46
Major and Minor 2nds: A Shortcut
Major and Minor 3rds: A Shortcut
Enharmonic Notes and Intervals
Mad Music Game: Name the 3rds
Theory Worksheet 48
Ear-Training Worksheet 49

Lesson 9

Learning Guide 50
  Major Triads
  Minor Triads
  A Closer Look at Triads
  Arpeggios
  The Sound of Descending Intervals: min 3,
    P5, P8
Theory Worksheet 53
Ear-Training Worksheet 54

Lesson 10

Learning Guide 55
  The Natural Minor Scale
  Relative Major and Minor Scales
  Sight Singing in Minor Keys
Theory Worksheet 56
Ear-Training Worksheet 57

Lesson 11

Learning Guide 58
  Two New Minor Scales: E Minor and B Minor
  Major and Minor Relatives
  How to Identify Relative Major and Minor Scales
Theory Worksheet 60
Ear-Training Worksheet 61

Lesson 12

Learning Guide 62
  Minor Key Signatures with Sharps
  Writing Minor Scales with a Key Signature
Theory Worksheet 63
Ear-Training Worksheet 65

Lesson 13

Learning Guide 66
  Two New Minor Scales: D Minor and G Minor
  Minor Key Signatures with Flats
  Writing Minor Scales with Accidentals
  Mad Music Game: Minor Key Signatures
Theory Worksheet 68
Ear-Training Worksheet 70

Lesson 14

Learning Guide 71
  A Closer Look at Dotted Notes
  New Rhythmic Unit ♩♩
  Rhythm Jumble Games
Theory Worksheet 72
Ear-Training Worksheet 73

Lesson 15

Learning Guide 74
  The Sound of the Descending Major 3rd and
    Perfect 4th
  Melodic Inversion
Theory Worksheet 76
Ear-Training Worksheet 78

Lesson 16

Learning Guide 79
  Italian Terms
  Tempo Markings
  Chromatic Notes
Theory Worksheet 81
Ear-Training Worksheet 82

Lesson 17

Learning Guide 84
  More Tempo Markings
  Tonic and Dominant Triads
Theory Worksheet 85
Ear-Training Worksheet 87

Lesson 18

Learning Guide 88
  The Sound of Descending Major and Minor
    2nds
  The Dotted Quarter-Note Beat
  Simple Time and Compound Time
Theory Worksheet 90
Ear-Training Worksheet 91

Lesson 19

Learning Guide 93
  A Closer Look at Minor Triads
  The Sound of the Descending Minor 6th
Theory Worksheet 95
Ear-Training Worksheet 97

Lesson 20

Learning Guide 99
  Learning a New Piece: What to Look for First
  Identifying the Key of a Melody:
    Major vs. Minor
  New Rhythmic Unit ♪♫
Theory Worksheet 101
Ear-Training Worksheet 103

Lesson 21

Learning Guide 105
  Musical Texture
  Polyphonic Texture
  Homophonic Texture
Theory Worksheet 107
Ear-Training Worksheet 109

Lesson 22

Learning Guide 110
  Review of Baroque and Classical Style
  Musical Style of the Romantic Period
Theory Worksheet 112
Ear-Training Worksheet 113

Lesson 23

Learning Guide 114
  A Closer Look at Romantic Musical Style: Art
    Song and Nationalism
  The Piano in the Romantic Period
Theory Worksheet 115
Ear-Training Worksheet 116

Lesson 24

Learning Guide 117
  The Romantic Orchestra
  Composers of the Romantic Period
Theory Worksheet 118
Ear-Training Worksheet 119

Theory Examination 120

Melody Master 125

Charts and Games

Rhythm Jumble Chart 129
Rhythm Jumble Games 130
Terms and Symbols Chart 131
Song Clue Chart 133
Mad Music Games 135

Answer Keys

Ear-Training 138
Melody Master 162
Mad Music 165

Appendix

Sight-Singing Syllable Systems 167

Preface for Teachers

Too often, music theory instruction emphasizes written concepts, with little attention paid to the way things actually *sound*. Our teaching philosophy is simple: never take the *sound* out of music theory instruction!

The *Sound Advice* program relates musical sounds to their symbols by combining written and aural theory. Throughout the series, theoretical concepts are introduced in a clear, concise manner and immediately reinforced with written worksheets and ear-training assignments. Students are also provided with lessons on musical style and an introduction to improvisation and composition.

Students of all instruments, including those who study voice, can use *Sound Advice*. Ideally, the program should be started under the guidance of a teacher as early as possible in a student's musical training. *Sound Advice* can be used successfully in private lessons, small group sessions, or in classroom teaching. On average, most private students will complete one lesson per week, while students in semester-long theory or musicianship classes may progress at a faster pace. Either way, the lesson planning is taken care of for teachers; each lesson is carefully organized so that students are presented with an appropriate amount of new material while continuing to review previously introduced concepts. Constant review is an important feature of *Sound Advice*.

Each *Sound Advice* lesson consists of a Learning Guide that introduces new material, a written Theory Worksheet, and an Ear-Training Worksheet to be completed using the accompanying CD. There are also a number of Charts and Games that reinforce material learned in the lessons.

Ear-training activities in Level 4 include sight singing of melodies and rhythms, rhythm singbacks and clapbacks, melody playbacks and singbacks, rhythmic and melodic dictation, identification of intervals, triads, scales, meters, and texture (homophonic or polyphonic), editing (error detection), and improvisation. Answers to all of the ear-training activities in *Sound Advice* can be checked by the student. We have provided Ear-Training Answer Keys so that students can mark their work at home immediately after completing each exercise. Teachers can easily monitor their students' ear-training progress by viewing the marked pages at the next lesson. Ear-training exercises can be repeated as many times as necessary for extra practice. Written Theory Worksheets are to be marked by the teacher.

It is important that teachers and students, as well as parents, understand the *How to Use This Book* section (pp. 7–9). For younger students, the teacher's guidance may be needed to get them started.

While *Sound Advice* can be used to prepare students for the ear-training and theory components of several major examining boards,[1] our main goal is to help *all* students become musically literate—to have a better understanding of how music "works" and to continue to develop a deeper appreciation for it throughout their lives.

Brenda Braaten and *Crystal Wiksyk*

---

[1] Level 4 covers ear-training requirements for The Royal Conservatory of Music (RCM) Grade 4 piano and voice examinations, Victoria Conservatory of Music (VCM) Grade 4 theory and musicianship examinations, and most Level 4 requirements of other examining boards and music teachers' associations. We strongly recommend that teachers consult current syllabi of specific examining boards for their requirements in each grade.

How to Use This Book

Lesson Organization

Each *Sound Advice* lesson contains three parts:

Learning Guide
The Learning Guides explain and illustrate new concepts. When you begin a lesson, always study the Learning Guide before completing the Theory Worksheet and the Ear-Training Worksheet.

Theory Worksheet
The Theory Worksheets contain written exercises for both new and review concepts. Your teacher will mark them for you when they are completed.

Ear-Training Worksheet
The Ear-Training Worksheets involve sight-singing melodies and rhythms, performing melody playbacks/singbacks and rhythm clapbacks/singbacks, completing dictation and improvisation activities, and identifying intervals, triads, arpeggios, homophonic and polyphonic textures, and duple and triple meters. Detailed instructions are provided below. You can check your answers to these assignments yourself, using the Ear-Training Answer Key at the back of the book.

Completing the Ear-Training Worksheets

You will need to go online to access the audio tracks for *Sound Advice* Level 4 to complete the Ear-Training Worksheets. In this book, the track numbers for each exercise are identified by an icon in the margin. The instructions for each exercise will be read aloud on the recording for the first three lessons only. Beginning with Lesson 4, you must read the instructions for each question yourself. Take time to read the instructions *before* you listen to the recorded examples.

For sight-singing and rhythmic-reading questions, you should pause the recording and perform each example by yourself first, tapping a steady quarter-note beat with your finger while you sing. To check your accuracy, sing the example a second time while listening to the recording and following along in the answer key.

For these activities, we recommend the use of syllables. Rhythm syllables are presented in the Learning Guides alongside new rhythmic concepts. For scales and melodies, we recommend movable do pitch syllables, but students should use whatever syllables work best for them. There is a description of the most common sight-singing syllable systems in the Appendix (pp. 167–168). In the Ear-Training Answer Key, rhythm syllables are given below all the rhythmic reading examples, and rhythm syllables are used on the recording. For sight-singing examples, because there are different options for movable do syllables when singing in a minor key (see p. 55), syllables are given only for examples in major keys. On the recording, examples in major keys are sung with syllables; examples in minor keys are played on the piano. When you are asked to sing an example that is out of your vocal range, you can sing it in a different octave, or internalize the sound (sing it in your head).

Sight-singing melodies and rhythms will be played once on the recording. All the other ear-training examples will be played twice, but you may re-play them as many times as necessary. On the Ear-Training Worksheets, you will be asked to record the number of times you listened. Your eventual goal is to complete each question after hearing the recorded example just twice.

When you finish an activity, turn immediately to the Ear-Training Answer Key to mark your work. *Do not erase your mistakes and replace them with the correct answers.* Instead, write in the correct answers *above* the errors. If you correct your work this way, you and your teacher will be able to look back at your progress over several lessons and identify areas that need extra practice.

Important: If you make any mistakes on an ear-training question, always go back and listen to the recorded example again to make sure you understand the correct answer.

How to Use This Book

Charts and Games

The Charts and Games begin on p. 129. The charts include Rhythm Jumble, Terms and Symbols, and Song Clue. These charts provide reinforcement for both writing and ear-training activities. Instructions on how to use each chart appear at the top of the chart.

The games include Rhythm Jumble Reading, Rhythm Jumble Solitaire, Rhythm Jumble Composer, and Mad Music. The games provide an opportunity for students to improve their facility in a fun setting. Instructions on how to play the games appear at the beginning of the Games section.

Suggestions for Daily Ear-Training Practice

Daily practice in ear training is essential to developing total musicianship. Even if you complete your ear-training assignment immediately after your lesson, you should still do a few minutes of ear-training practice every day until your next lesson. If for some reason you finish *Sound Advice* Level 4 but have to wait before you start Level 5, you should continue to practice ear training every day.

Here are some suggestions:

Sing Intervals

One easy way to learn intervals is to relate them to the notes of the major scale. For example, to learn the perfect 5th, sing up the first five notes of a major scale, stop on the fifth note, then sing the first note again. Sing those two notes back and forth to memorize the sound of that interval.

Song clues can be helpful for identifying and singing intervals. On pp. 133–134, there is a chart showing the ascending and descending intervals with several song clue examples. There is also space for you to add your own song clues. If you sing or hum the song clues, you will quickly memorize the sound of the intervals.

Another way to practice singing intervals is to use the Play–Hear–Sing–Play method. Follow these four steps:
1) Play the first note of the interval on your instrument.
2) Hear the second note in your mind. (Use a song clue or relate the notes to the major scale.)
3) Sing the second note out loud.
4) Play the second note on your instrument to see if you sang the right pitch.

Sing Rhythms

One of the best ways to practice rhythm is to use the music you are currently playing or singing. Choose a passage to work on, tap the beat (eventually you will *feel* the beat in your body), and play or sing the rhythms. Be sure to feel the regular accent of the time signature. Remember, the goal is to recognize the symbols on the page as familiar patterns of sounds—not to count them out. Regular practice in this manner will greatly improve your sight reading.

You can also use the Rhythm Jumble Chart on p. 129 to practice singing rhythms every day.

How to Use This Book

Play by Ear
Try to play familiar melodies on your instrument without reading from the music. To determine which note of the scale a melody starts on, sing the tune and hold the *last* note, which may well be the first note of the scale ($\hat{1}$). Now compare that last note to the first note of the melody. Are the pitches the same or different? How far apart are they? HINT: Many familiar melodies begin on the fifth scale degree ($\hat{5}$), for example, *Happy Birthday, Silent Night, Here Comes the Bride, Oh Christmas Tree,* and *Amazing Grace.*

Familiar Tune Dictation
Try writing out a familiar melody. To figure out the meter, sing the tune while you tap the beat and listen for the regular accents. To find which note of the scale the melody begins and ends on, use the same procedure described under Play by Ear. If you can sing the tune using pitch syllables, you should be able to write it starting on any note you choose. Compare your written version with the printed music if you have a copy.

Extra Sight Singing
You can use the Ear-Training Answer Key for extra practice in singing melodies and rhythms. When you sight sing these "answers," follow the same procedure you use when reading melodies and rhythms on the ear-training assignments.

Lesson 1

Learning Guide

I am your Professor. I will be your guide throughout this book.

Be sure to follow my advice when I offer you a suggestion!

Review of Note Values and Rests

Here are all the note values and rests you learned in previous levels of *Sound Advice*.

Name	Symbol	Quarter-Note Beats	Symbol for Rest
Whole Note	𝅝	4	𝄻
Half Note	𝅗𝅥	2	𝄼
Quarter Note	♩	1	𝄽
Eighth Note	♪	$\frac{1}{2}$	𝄾
Sixteenth Note	𝅘𝅥𝅯	$\frac{1}{4}$	𝄿

Note-Value Comparison Chart

This chart shows how all these notes relate to each other. Two notes of the same value are always equal in length to the next longer note.

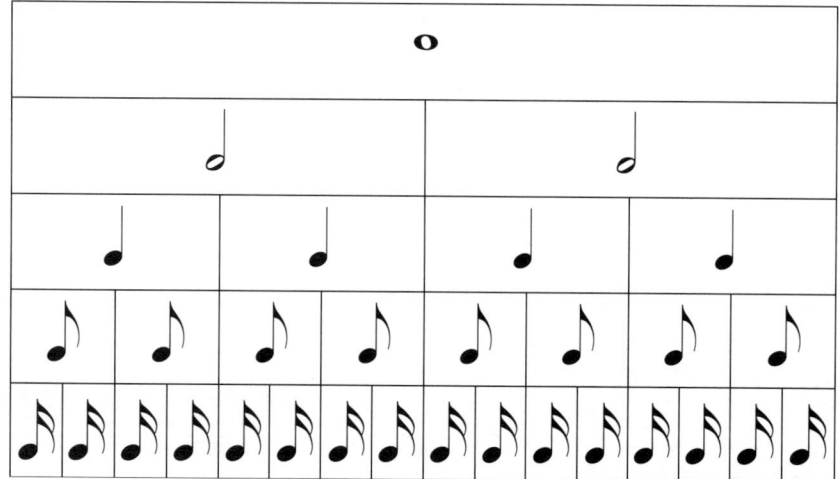

Ties and Dots

In the following examples, the quarter note is equal to one beat.

A **tie** joins two notes together into one continuous sound. The length of the sound is equal to the total length of the two notes.

For example: 𝅝 ⌣ 𝅗𝅥 = 6 beats

𝅗𝅥 ⌣ 𝅘𝅥 = 3 beats

𝅘𝅥 ⌣ 𝅘𝅥𝅮 = 1½ beats

𝅘𝅥𝅮 ⌣ 𝅘𝅥𝅯 = ¾ beat

A **dot** lengthens a note by one half of its original value.

For example: 𝅝. = 𝅝 ⌣ 𝅗𝅥 
$\quad\quad\quad$ 4 + 2 $\quad$ = 6 beats

𝅗𝅥. = 𝅗𝅥 ⌣ 𝅘𝅥
$\quad\quad$ 2 + 1 $\quad$ = 3 beats

𝅘𝅥. = 𝅘𝅥 ⌣ 𝅘𝅥𝅮
$\quad\quad$ 1 + ½ $\quad$ = 1½ beats

𝅘𝅥𝅮. = 𝅘𝅥𝅮 ⌣ 𝅘𝅥𝅯
$\quad\quad$ ½ + ¼ $\quad$ = ¾ beat

LESSON 1 Learning Guide

Beaming Notes to Show the Beat

Single eighth notes and sixteenth notes have flags. A group of several eighth notes or sixteenth notes can be beamed together to show the quarter-note beat. This makes the rhythm easier to read.

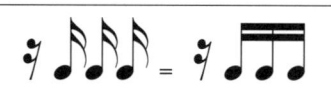

Rhythmic Reading

Musicians "feel" the beat when they perform music. A good way to practice this skill is to tap a steady beat while you sing rhythmic patterns.

Sing the following rhythmic units while you tap a steady quarter-note beat. Repeat each unit several times before you move on to the next one.

Sing:	ta - a - a - a	ta - a - a	ta - a	ta	ti ti	ti ka ti ka	ti ti ka	ti ka ti
Tap:	x x x x	x x x	x x	x	x x	x	x	x

These two units sound the same:

Sing: ta - m ti
Tap: x x

Sing: ta - m ti
Tap: x x

The eighth notes are pronounced "tee."

The sixteenth notes are pronounced "tih."

When you sing a rhythmic pattern, you can be silent on the rests, but continue to tap the quarter-note beat.

Sing:	sh - sh - sh - sh	sh - sh	sh	sh ti	sh ka ti ka
Tap:	x x x x	x x	x	x	x

12   Lesson 1 Learning Guide   Sound Advice Level 4

Learning Guide

One-Minute Rhythm Jumble

On p. 129, you will find the Rhythm Jumble sight-reading chart. Each time you learn a new rhythmic unit, circle it on this chart. You can circle all the rhythmic units you reviewed in this lesson.

Use the Rhythm Jumble Chart to practice rhythms for *one minute* every day. Tap the quarter-note beat with your finger as you point to the rhythmic unit you are singing. Sing each unit two or three times before you move on to the next one. Gradually mix the rhythms up by randomly pointing to different units. Do this for one minute. Try not to miss a beat.

LESSON 1: Theory Worksheet

1 Complete the following note-value comparison chart. The first row has been done for you.

Name	Symbol
whole note	𝅝

2 Fill in the blanks. Refer to the note-value comparison chart above if you need help.

8 sixteenth notes = _____ eighth note(s)

6 eighth notes   = _____ quarter note(s)

4 eighth notes   = _____ quarter note(s)

8 sixteenth notes = _____ half note(s)

16 sixteenth notes = _____ half note(s)

3 Rewrite the following rhythm, beaming the eighth notes and sixteenth notes to show the quarter-note beats.

Rewrite here:

4 Draw a line to connect each group of notes on the left with its corresponding note value on the right.

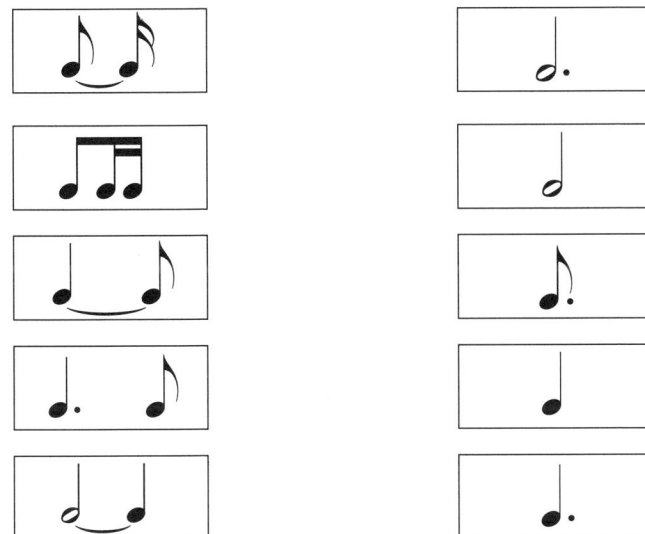

5 One-Minute Rhythm Jumble: Record the number of days you practiced. ☐

LESSON 1
Ear-Training Worksheet

Before you begin the Ear-Training Worksheets, turn to p. 7 and read the instructions.

1) Rhythmic Reading:

a) Pause the recording. Sing the following rhythmic patterns while you tap a steady quarter-note beat.

b) Turn to the answer key and sing along with the recording.

Stop! Sing them by yourself first!

2) Rhythmic Reading:

a) Pause the recording. Sing the following rhythmic pattern while you tap a steady quarter-note beat.

b) Turn to the answer key and sing along with the recording.

3) Rhythm Singback/Clapback: Sing, tap, or clap the rhythmic pattern you hear from memory. The pattern will be played twice but you may listen as many times as you need. Record the number of times you listened. That will be your score.

Always tap the beat while you listen.

Ear-Training Worksheet

LESSON 1

4 **Rhythm Singback/Clapback:** Sing, tap, or clap the rhythmic pattern you hear from memory. The pattern will be played twice but you may listen as many times as you need.

5 **Rhythmic Identification:** Identify the correct notation for the rhythmic pattern you hear. Each pattern will be played twice.

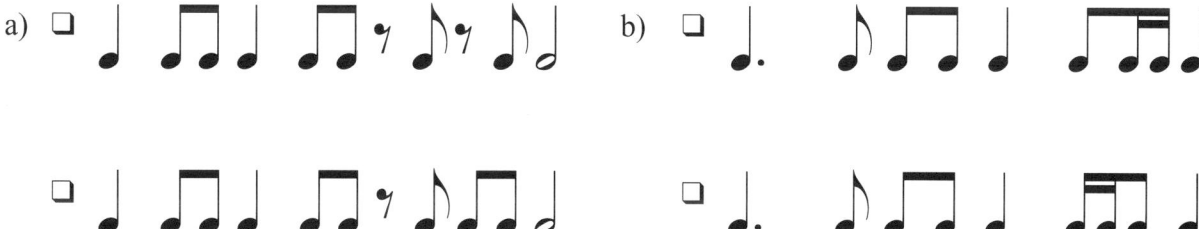

Sound Advice Level 4   Lesson 1 Ear-Training Worksheet   17

Learning Guide

Half Steps and Whole Steps

On a keyboard, a **half step** ($\frac{1}{2}$) or **semitone** is the distance from one key to the very next key, whether that key is black or white.

Remember the saying "Bach Composed Every Friday" to help you remember the white-key half steps.

A **whole step** (W) or **whole tone** is made up of two half steps. On a keyboard, there is one key between the two notes of a whole step. The key can be either black or white.

Accidentals

Accidentals are symbols that alter the pitch of a note.

A **sharp** (♯) raises the pitch of a note by one half step.

A **flat** (♭) lowers the pitch of a note by one half step.

A **natural** (♮) cancels a previous sharp or flat.

Remember these points when you write accidentals:

- Place accidentals in *front* of a note.
- Place accidentals on the same line or space as the notehead.
- Accidentals affect *only* the pitch of the note that they are in front of. For example, a sharp on Middle C does not affect any other C on the staff.
- An accidental is cancelled by a bar line.
- If you want to cancel an accidental before the next bar line, use a natural sign.

Here are some examples of accidentals.

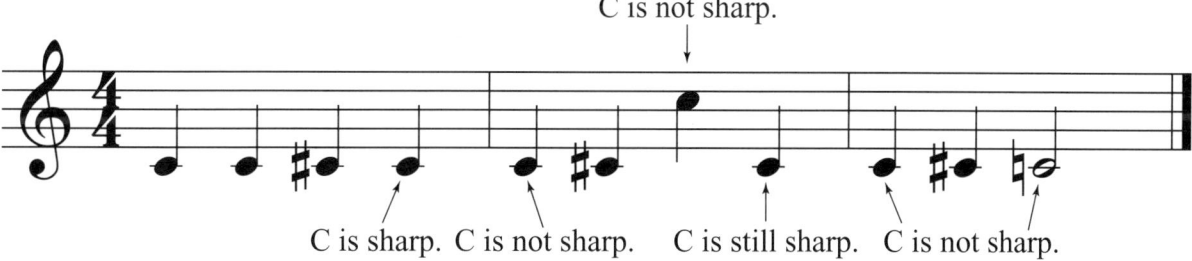

Enharmonic Equivalents

A pitch can have at least two different spellings. For example, G♯ and A♭ represent the same black key on a piano keyboard. These two notes are **enharmonic equivalents**.

G♯ or A♭

LESSON 2 Learning Guide

Major Scale Review: C, G, D, F, and B♭ Major

Major scales can start on any note. All major scales have a similar sound because of the pattern of whole steps and half steps: W W ½ W W W ½.

Here are the major scales you have learned so far:

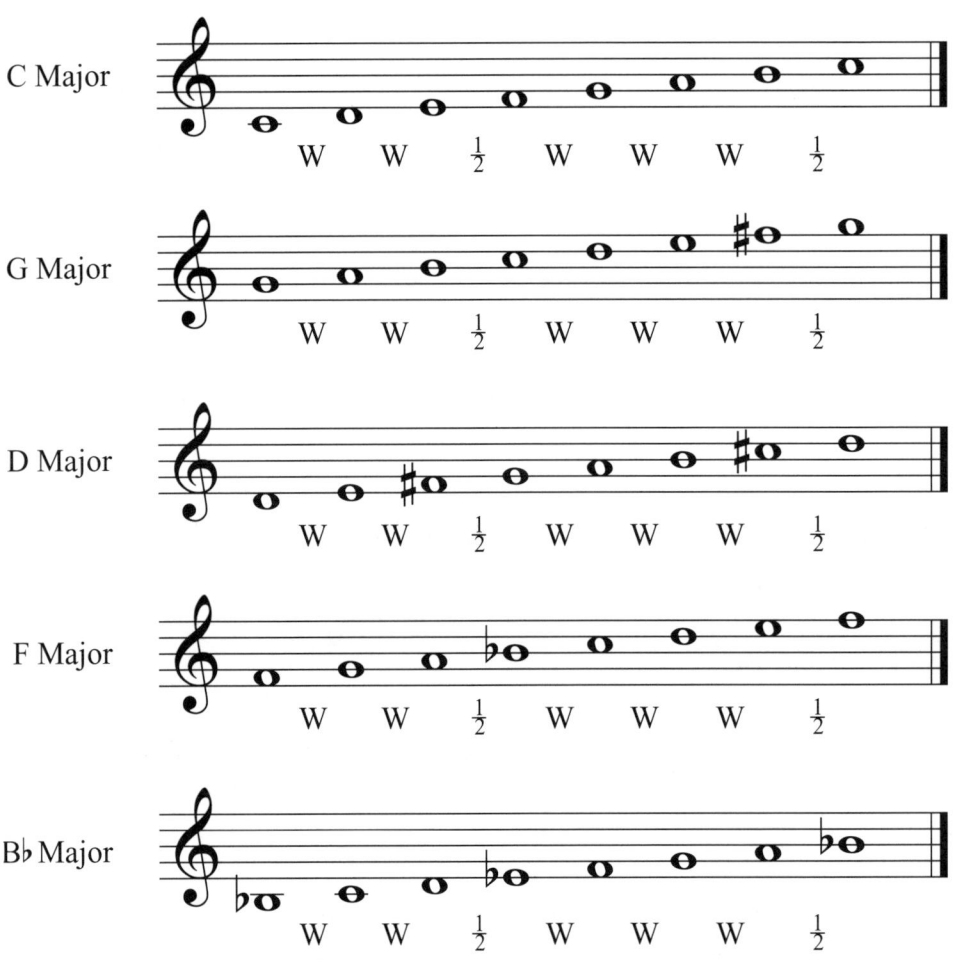

Accidentals are needed to maintain the pattern of whole and half steps.

The best way to learn the sound of the major scale is to sing it out loud. We recommend using pitch syllables when you sing scales and melodies. Your teacher may suggest a different method for sight singing. (For a description of the most common syllable systems, see pp. 167–168.)

Scale Degree Numbers

Each scale tone has a number. A carat sign (^) above a number identifies that number as a scale degree. The first note of a scale is always $\hat{1}$ no matter where it is placed on the staff.

The following melody is based on the C major scale:

Theory Worksheet — LESSON 2

1 On the keyboard below, draw a curved arrow from each note marked ✗ to the note a whole (W) step *higher* in pitch. The first one has been done for you.

2 On the keyboard below, draw a curved arrow from each note marked ✗ to the note a half (½) step *lower* in pitch. The first one has been done for you.

3 Draw curved arrows on the keyboard below to create a D major scale. The first arrow has been done for you. When you are finished, play the scale you have written.

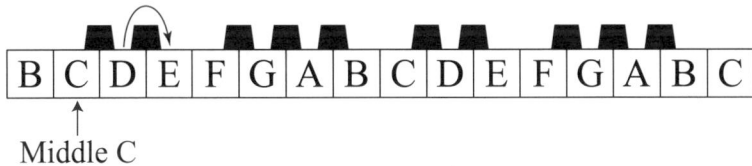

Middle C

4 Using the keyboard above as a guide, write a D major scale on the staff below. Use accidentals instead of a key signature.

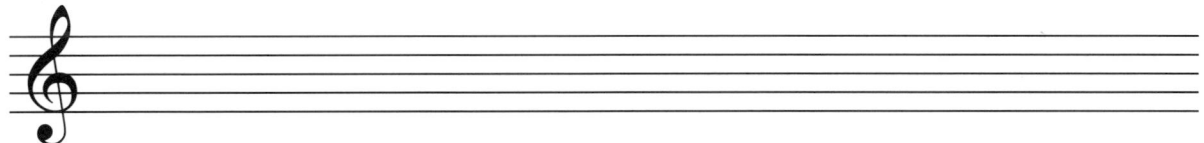

5 Draw a line to connect each note on the left with its enharmonic equivalent on the right.

C♯	A♯
F♯	D♭
B♭	F
E♯	G♭

6 One-Minute Rhythm Jumble: Record the number of days you practiced. ☐

Sound Advice Level 4 — Lesson 2 Theory Worksheet

LESSON 2 — Ear-Training Worksheet

1 Editing: You will hear five pairs of notes. The first note of each pair will be played as written. Based on what you hear, add a sharp, flat, or natural to the *second* note. Each pair of notes will be played twice.

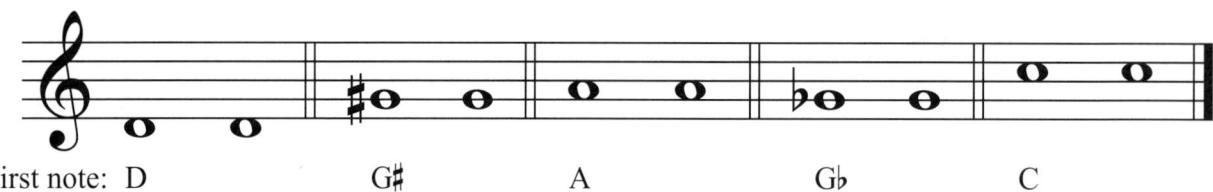

First note: D   G♯   A   G♭   C

2 Rhythmic Identification: Identify the correct notation for the rhythmic pattern you hear. Each pattern will be played twice.

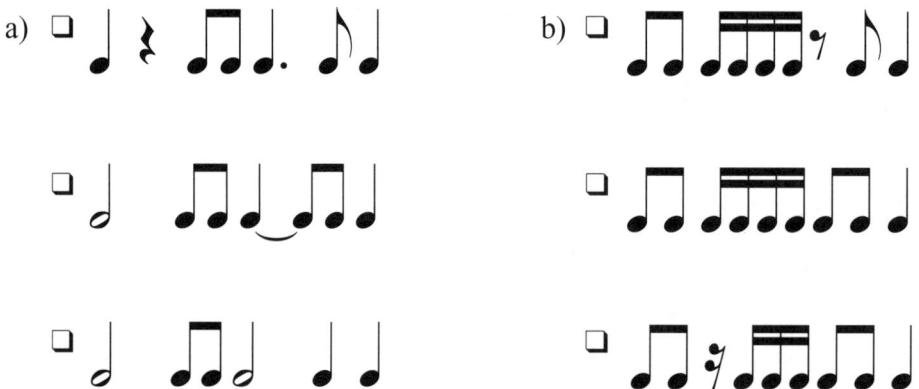

3 Rhythm Singback/Clapback: Sing, tap, or clap the rhythmic pattern you hear from memory. The pattern will be played twice but you may listen as many times as you need.

I LISTENED ☐ TIMES

4 Sight Singing:
a) Pause the recording. Sing a C major scale, ascending and descending.
b) Turn to the answer key and sing along with the recording.

5 Sight Singing:
a) Pause the recording. Sing the following melody while you tap a steady quarter-note beat.
b) Turn to the answer key and sing along with the recording.

Learning Guide — Lesson 3

Key Signatures

When a piece of music uses the notes from a particular scale, it is said to be in the **key** of that scale. For example, the melody below uses notes of the B♭ major scale. Therefore, it is in the key of B♭ major, and the tonic is B♭.

The sharps or flats needed for the key of a piece can be grouped at the beginning of each line of music as a **key signature**.

The sharps or flats in a key signature affect *all* pitches with that letter name. For example, a B♭ in the key signature means that all B's should be played as B♭. The example below has a key signature of two flats.

Key Signature Shortcuts

Here are two shortcuts you can use to figure out the number of sharps or flats in the key signature of a given key.

For sharp keys: Count up in 5ths. For example, the key signature of C major has no sharps. The key signature of G major (which is a 5th higher) has one sharp. The key signature of D major has two sharps, and so on.

The sharps in a key signature always appear on the staff in the order and position shown in the example below. Notice that the order of sharps also goes up by 5ths:

F♯ ⟶ C♯ ⟶ and so on
 P5   P5

For sharps, say "Fat Cats."

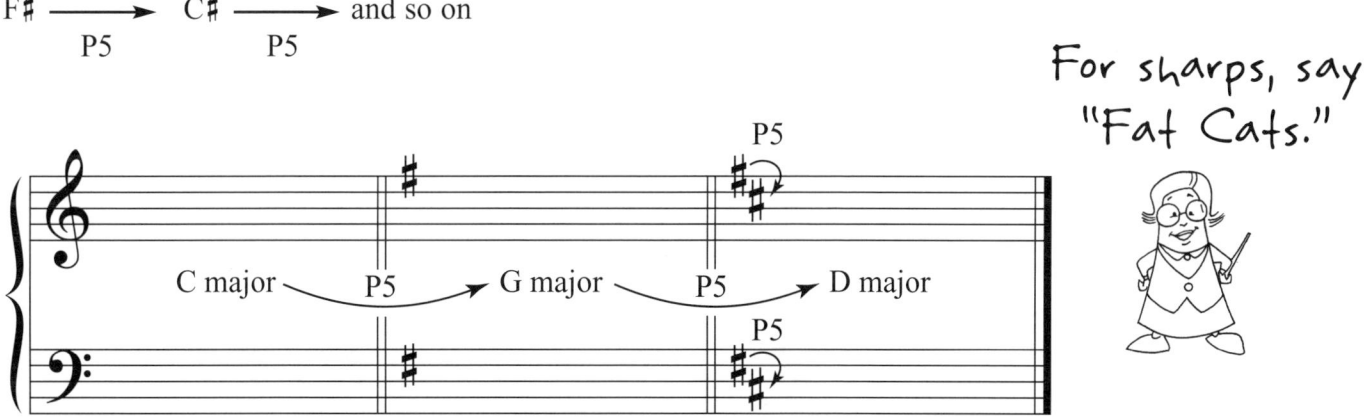

Sound Advice Level 4 — Lesson 3 Learning Guide — 23

LESSON 3: Learning Guide

For flat keys: Count up in 4ths. For example, the key signature of C major has no flats. The key signature of F major (which is a 4th higher) has one flat. The key signature of B♭ major has two flats, and so on.

The flats in a key signature always appear on the staff in the order and position shown in the example below. Notice that the order of flats also goes up by 4ths:

B♭ ⟶ E♭ ⟶ and so on
   P4   P4

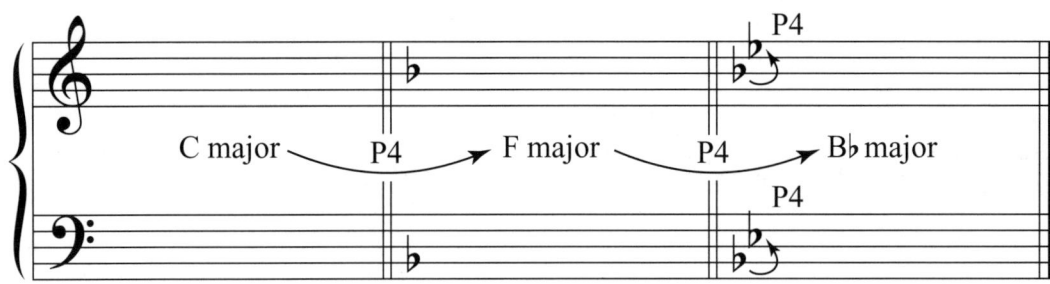

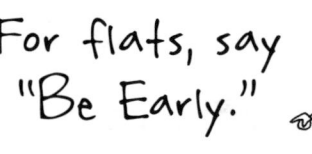

For flats, say "Be Early."

Mad Music Game: Major Key Signatures

From now on, many of your Theory Worksheets will include spaces for you to record three Mad Music scores. This means that part of your homework assignment for that lesson is to play Mad Music at least three times. For the Mad Music instructions, see p. 135.

The first Mad Music game involves key signatures. The Mad Music Key Signature Chart is on p. 136. Your goal is to accurately name all the major key signatures on the chart in 20 seconds or less. Try to achieve this goal before you begin Lesson 8.

Theory Worksheet

LESSON 3

1 Identify the following pairs of notes as either whole steps (W) or half steps ($\frac{1}{2}$).

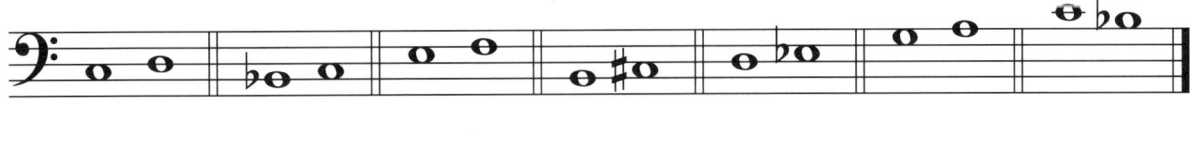

___ ___ ___ ___ ___ ___ ___

2 Write the pattern of whole steps and half steps in a major scale.

___ ___ ___ ___ ___ ___ ___

3 Draw curved arrows on the following keyboard to create a B♭ major scale. The first one has been done for you.

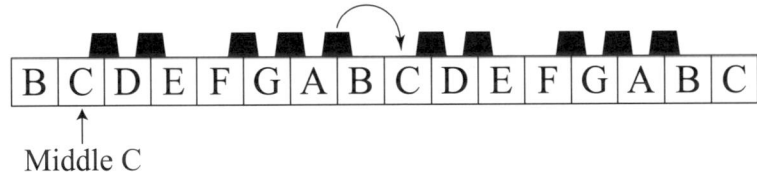

Middle C

4 Using the above keyboard as a guide, write a B♭ major scale in whole notes on the staff below. Use a key signature instead of accidentals.

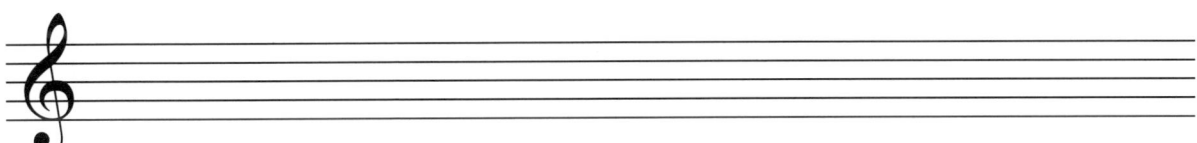

5 Write the following key signatures on the grand staff below.

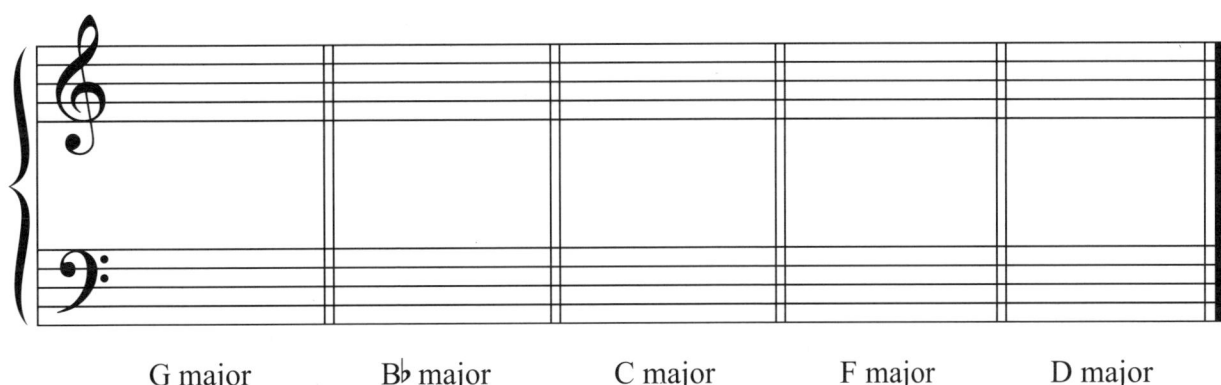

G major   B♭ major   C major   F major   D major

6 Mad Music Scores ☐ ☐ ☐

Sound Advice Level 4 — Lesson 3 Theory Worksheet

LESSON 3
Ear-Training Worksheet

 1 **Rhythmic Identification:** Identify the correct notation for the rhythmic pattern you hear. Each pattern will be played twice.

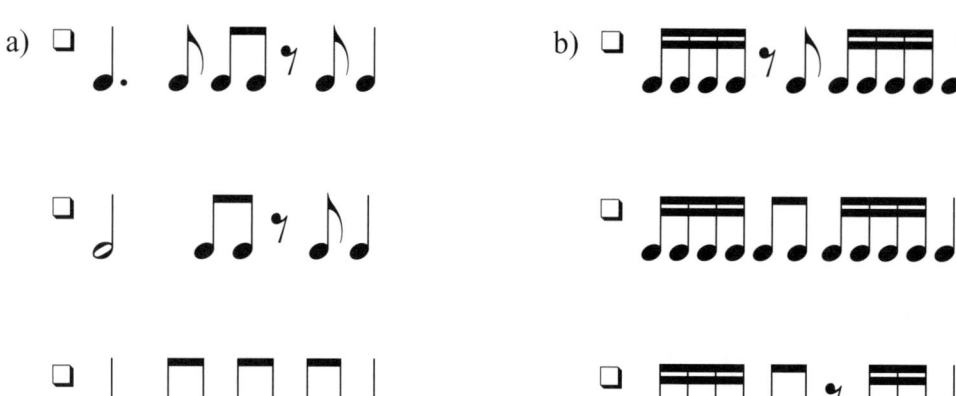

 2 **Rhythm Singback/Clapback:** Sing, tap, or clap the rhythmic pattern you hear from memory. The pattern will be played twice but you may listen as many times as you need.

I LISTENED ☐ TIMES

 3 **Sight Singing:**
  a) Pause the recording. Sing a D major scale, ascending and descending.
  b) Turn to your answer key and sing along with the recording.

 4 **Sight Singing:**
  a) Pause the recording. Sing the following melody while you tap a steady quarter-note beat.
  b) Turn to the answer key and sing along with the recording.

 5 **Melody Singback/Playback:** Sing the melody you hear from memory, then play it back on your instrument. The melody is in C major. It will be played twice.

I LISTENED ☐ TIMES

Learning Guide

Meter and Time Signatures

A repeating pattern of strong and weak beats is called a **meter**. A **time signature** identifies the meter of a piece of music.

A time signature is written at the beginning of a piece. When the pattern of regular beats changes in the middle of a piece of music, a new time signature is needed.

When you write or identify a time signature, remember these four points:

- The top number of a time signature tells you the number of beats in each measure—that is, the type of meter.
- The bottom number of a time signature tells you what kind of note gets one beat.
- A time signature should never look like a fraction.

$$\begin{matrix} \mathbf{2} \\ \mathbf{4} \end{matrix} \qquad \dfrac{\mathbf{2}}{\mathbf{4}}$$

Correct   Incorrect

- On the grand staff, the time signature appears in both staves. The time signature always goes *after* the key signature.

Here are the meters and time signatures you have learned so far, and the symbols for their accent patterns.

Accent pattern symbols: Strong (ʳ)   weak (˘)   Medium (–)

Duple Meter	Triple Meter	Quadruple Meter
$\frac{2}{4}$ = $\frac{2}{♩}$	$\frac{3}{4}$ = $\frac{3}{♩}$	$\frac{4}{4}$ = $\frac{4}{♩}$
ʳ ˘	ʳ ˘ ˘	ʳ ˘ – ˘

$\frac{4}{4}$ is also called **common time**. The symbol **C** is an abbreviation for common time.

Sound Advice Level 4   Lesson 4 Learning Guide   27

LESSON 4 Learning Guide

Adding Time Signatures and Bar Lines

If the bottom number of a time signature is 4, the beat is based on the quarter note. When you are asked to add time signatures or bar lines in your Theory Worksheets, start by circling the quarter-note beats, as shown in the following example.

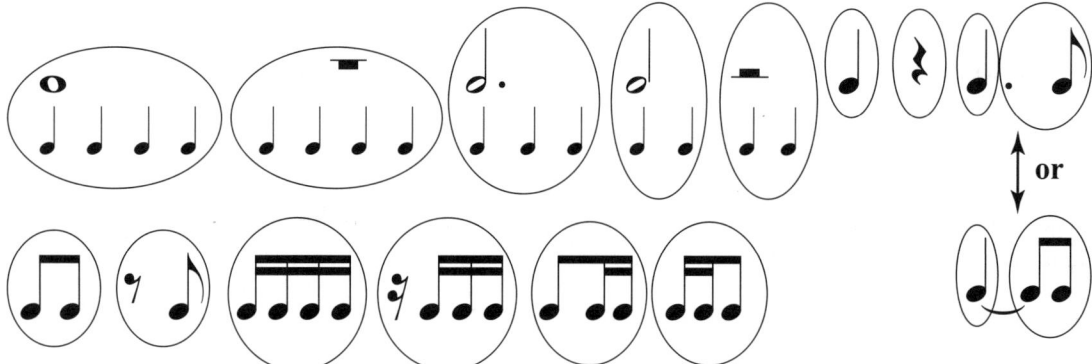

Rhythmic Dictation

Writing down—or notating—what you hear is called dictation. When you do rhythmic dictation, you only write the rhythm, even if the example you hear is a melody.

You may be asked to write a rhythmic pattern as you listen to it, or to memorize the pattern first and then write it down from memory. If you have memorized the pattern, you can sing it to yourself as you write it down.

Follow these steps when you do either kind of rhythmic dictation. Try this example:

1 Write a stem for each sound you hear. Write the stems close together when you hear short notes, and farther apart when you hear longer notes.

2 Sing the pattern back to yourself from memory while you follow the stems you have written. Try to remember which notes were longer and which were shorter. Add the notehead for the dotted half note and beams on the eighth and sixteenth notes.

3 Add noteheads to the other stems to complete your dictation. If you are not working from memory, you may need to listen to the pattern several more times.

Theory Worksheet — Lesson 4

1 Circle the quarter-note beats in the following example, then add the correct time signature. Write the accent pattern above each measure.

2 Circle the quarter-note beats, then write the time signature in the treble staff and the bass staff.

3 Circle the quarter-note beats. Add bar lines according to the time signatures.

a)

b)

Don't forget to use double bar lines at the end!

4 Draw a line to connect each note on the left with its enharmonic equivalent on the right.

G♭	A♯
C♯	C
E	F♯
B♭	D♭
B♯	F♭

5 One-Minute Rhythm Jumble: Record the number of days you practiced. ☐

6 Mad Music Scores ☐ ☐ ☐

Sound Advice Level 4 — Lesson 4 Theory Worksheet

LESSON 4
Ear-Training Worksheet

Beginning with this lesson, the instructions will no longer be read aloud on the recording. Be sure to read each question carefully before you listen.

1. Sight Singing:

a) Pause the recording. Sing an F major scale, ascending and descending.

b) Turn to the answer key and sing along with the recording.

2. Sight Singing:

a) Pause the recording. Sing the following melody while you tap a steady quarter-note beat.

b) Turn to the answer key and sing along with the recording.

3. Rhythmic Reading:

a) Pause the recording. Sing the following rhythmic pattern while you tap a steady quarter-note beat.

b) Turn to the answer key and sing along with the recording.

4. Rhythm Singback/Clapback: Sing, tap, or clap the rhythmic pattern you hear from memory. It is in $\frac{2}{4}$ time.

LESSON 4
Ear-Training Worksheet

Track 20

5 **Rhythmic Dictation:** Write the rhythmic pattern you hear in the space below. Listen as many times as you need. The rhythm is in 2/4 time.

Write it down as you hear it!

Track 21

6 **Meter Identification:** Identify the meter of the following examples as either duple or triple.

a) ❑ duple   b) ❑ duple
   ❑ triple   ❑ triple

Tap the beat as you listen!

Sound Advice Level 4   Lesson 4 Ear-Training Worksheet   31

Learning Guide

Naming Major and Perfect Intervals

An **interval** is the distance between two notes. The name of an interval tells you two things: the *size* (shown with a number) and the *quality* (shown with a word: major, minor, or perfect).

To identify the size and quality of an interval:

1) Count the distance from one note to the other. Include both the lower note and the higher note in the total.
2) Identify the scale that begins on the lower note (in this case, C major). Think in this key.
3) Determine whether the upper note also belongs to this key. Intervals that belong to the major key of the bottom note are named as follows:

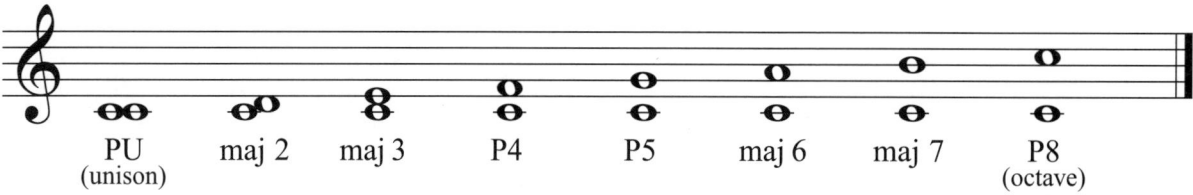

Unisons, 4ths, 5ths, and 8ves are **perfect** intervals. Perfect intervals are symbolized with "P" plus the size of the interval: PU, P4, P5, and P8.

The other intervals—2nds, 3rds, 6ths, and 7ths—are **major** intervals. Major intervals are symbolized with "maj" plus the size: maj 2, maj 3, maj 6, and maj 7.

The Sound of Ascending Intervals

In Level 4, you will review all the intervals covered in previous *Sound Advice* levels, and learn several new ones.

Here are the ascending intervals you have learned so far:

- major 2nd (maj 2)
- major 3rd (maj 3)
- perfect 4th (P4)
- perfect 5th (P5)
- major 6th (maj 6)
- major 7th (maj 7)
- perfect octave (P8)

Learning Guide 5

One way to memorize the sound of ascending intervals is to sing up from the first note of a major scale, as shown below:

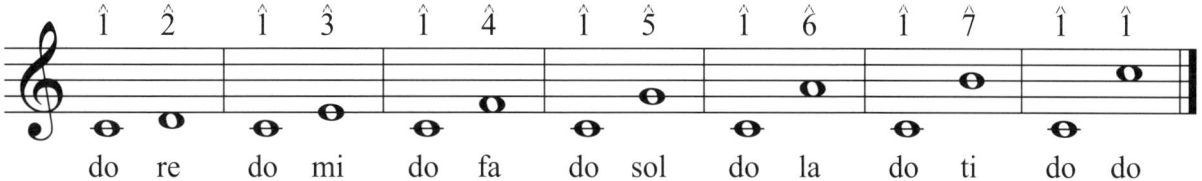

You might also also find it helpful to relate each interval to a familiar song. The Song Clue Chart on p. 133 lists song clues for all the intervals that are covered in Level 4. There is also space for you to write in your own songs.

Each time you learn or review an interval, put a ✔ beside it on the Song Clue Chart.

The Ascending Perfect 4th (P4)

The perfect 4th in the example at the top of this page is between $\hat{1}$ and $\hat{4}$ (do and fa). However, most melodies that begin with an ascending perfect 4th start on $\hat{5}$ and go up to $\hat{1}$ (sol up to do). Play or sing the example below.

On the Song Clue Chart, all the melodies listed for the ascending perfect 4th begin on $\hat{5}$ and go up to $\hat{1}$ (sol up to do).

The Ascending Major 6th (maj 6)

The major 6th in the example at the top of this page is between $\hat{1}$ and $\hat{6}$ (do up to la). However, most melodies that begin with an ascending major 6th start on $\hat{5}$ and go up to $\hat{3}$ (sol up to mi). Play or sing the example below.

On the Song Clue Chart, all the melodies listed for the ascending major 6th begin on $\hat{5}$ and go up to $\hat{3}$ (sol up to mi).

For additional ear-training practice tips, see "Suggestions for Daily Ear-Training Practice" on p. 8.

LESSON 5 Theory Worksheet

1. For each interval, answer the questions, then write the full name of the interval in the space provided. The first one has been done for you.

What size is this interval? ___7___

What major scale begins on the bottom note? _D major_

Does the upper note belong to this key? ___yes___

Interval name: ___maj 7___

What size is this interval? _____

What major scale begins on the bottom note? _____

Does the upper note belong to this key? _____

Interval name: _____

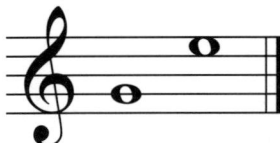

What size is this interval? _____

What major scale begins on the bottom note? _____

Does the upper note belong to this key? _____

Interval name: _____

What size is this interval? _____

What major scale begins on the bottom note? _____

Does the upper note belong to this key? _____

Interval name: _____

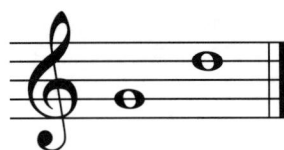

What size is this interval? _____

What major scale begins on the bottom note? _____

Does the upper note belong to this key? _____

Interval name: _____

2. One-Minute Rhythm Jumble: Record the number of days you practiced.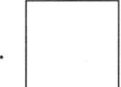

Ear-Training Worksheet — LESSON 5

 Track 22

1 Sight Singing:

a) Pause the recording. Sing a G major scale, ascending and descending.

b) Turn to the answer key and sing along with the recording.

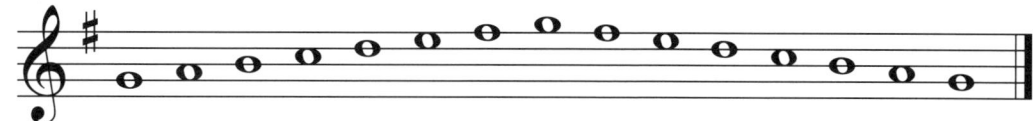

 Track 23

2 Sight Singing:

a) Pause the recording. Sing the following melody while you tap a steady quarter-note beat.

b) Turn to the answer key and sing along with the recording.

 Track 24

3 Interval Identification: Identify the intervals you hear as ↗ maj 2, maj 3, P4, P5, maj 6, maj 7, or P8.

a)   b)   c)   d)   e)

f)   g)   h)   i)   j)

 Track 25

4 Rhythm Clapback: Clap the *rhythm* of the melody you hear from memory. Your goal is to memorize the rhythm after the melody is played twice. Record the number of times you listened.

 Track 26

5 Melody Singback/Playback: Sing the melody you hear from memory, then play it on your instrument. The melody is in the key of F major, in 2/4 time.

Lesson 6 Learning Guide

Naming Minor Intervals

When the upper note of a major interval is lowered by a half step, the quality of the interval changes from major to minor. **Minor** intervals are symbolized with "min" and the size: min 2, min 3, min 6, min 7.

Important: Remember that only major intervals—2nds, 3rds, 6ths, and 7ths—can be changed to minor intervals. Perfect intervals—4ths, 5ths, and 8ves— do not become minor intervals.

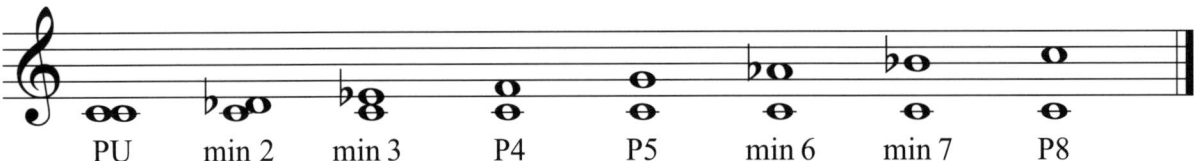

The Sound of Ascending Minor 2nds and 3rds

One way to learn the sound of minor 2nds and 3rds is to compare them to major 2nds and 3rds.

Sing and play the following major and minor 2nds. Compare the two different sounds.

Sing and play the following major and minor 3rds. Compare the two different sounds.

Learning Guide — Lesson 6

A Closer Look at Ascending Minor 2nds and 3rds

When you compared minor 2nds and 3rds to major 2nds and 3rds, you sang up from the first note of a major scale ($\hat{1}$).

In melodies, however, ascending minor 2nds and 3rds often start on other scale degrees. Let's take a look.

Ascending Minor 2nd

The ascending minor 2nd is often heard at the *end* of a melody, between $\hat{7}$ and $\hat{1}$ (ti and do). The minor 2nd gives these last two notes a "final" sound, as if the melody has arrived at its destination.

Sing or play the following melody and listen closely to the last two notes.

F major   ti do

Ascending minor 2nds are usually found at the end of a melody, but the Song Clue Chart lists a few songs that begin with this interval.

Ascending Minor 3rd

Sing the following melody.

C major mi   sol

The interval between $\hat{3}$ and $\hat{5}$ (mi to sol) is a minor 3rd. In major keys, when a melody begins with an ascending minor 3rd it usually starts on $\hat{3}$. Many familiar melodies begin like this.

Turn to the Song Clue Chart on p. 133 and put a ✔ beside the ascending minor 2nd (min 2) and the ascending minor 3rd (min 3).

LESSON 6 — Theory Worksheet

1 For each interval, answer the questions, then write the full name of the interval in the space provided. The first one has been done for you.

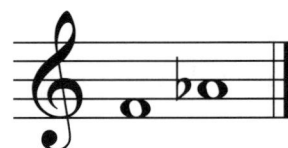

What size is this interval? __3rd__
What major scale begins on the bottom note? __F major__
Does the upper note belong to this key or is it a half step lower? __½ step lower__
Interval name: __min 3__

What size is this interval? _____
What major scale begins on the bottom note? _____
Does the upper note belong to this key or is it a half step lower? _____
Interval name: _____

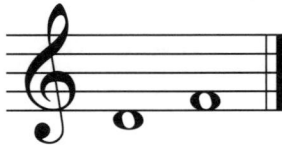

What size is this interval? _____
What major scale begins on the bottom note? _____
Does the upper note belong to this key or is it a half step lower? _____
Interval name: _____

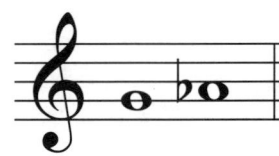

What size is this interval? _____
What major scale begins on the bottom note? _____
Does the upper note belong to this key or is it a half step lower? _____
Interval name: _____

2 Turn the following major intervals into minor intervals by adding an accidental to the upper note.

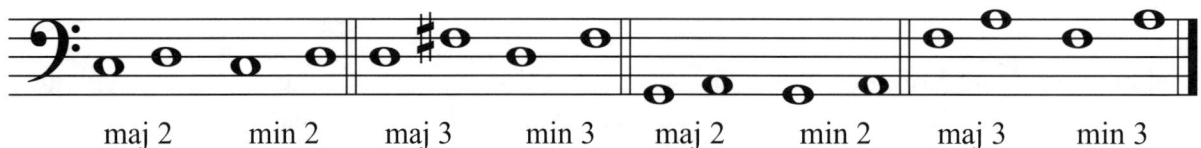

3 Circle the quarter-note beats, then add the correct time signature to each example.

4 Mad Music Scores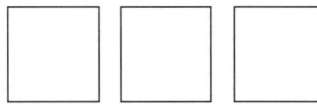

Ear-Training Worksheet

LESSON 6

 1 **Sight Singing:**
   a) Pause the recording. Sing the following melody while you tap a steady quarter-note beat.
   b) Turn to the answer key and sing along with the recording.

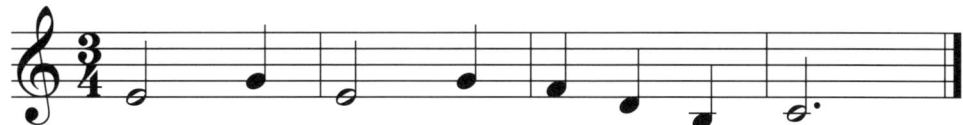

 2 **Interval Identification:** Identify the intervals you hear as min 2, maj 2, min 3, or maj 3.

a)   b)   c)   d)   e)   f)   g)

 3 **Editing:** The following intervals are written as major 2nds or 3rds. If you hear a major interval on the recording, leave the interval as written. If you hear a minor interval, add the appropriate accidental to the upper note.

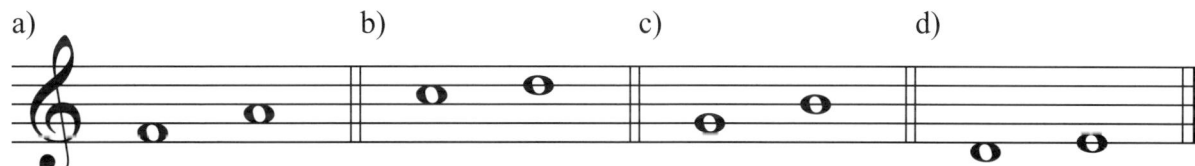

 4 **Melodic Dictation:** Add the missing notes under the bracket. The melody will be played twice.

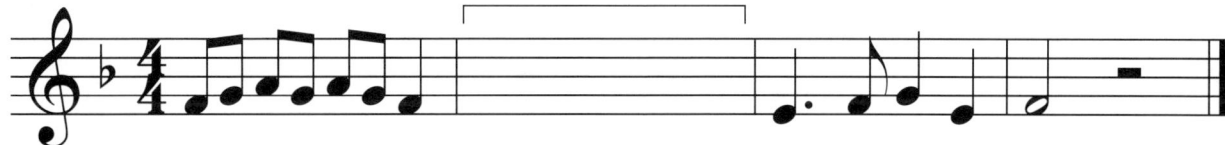

 5 **Rhythmic Dictation:** Write the rhythmic pattern you hear in the space below. Listen as many times as you need. The rhythm is in 3/4 time.

Write it down as you hear it!

Learning Guide

Incomplete Measures

Some melodies begin on the first beat of the measure, the **downbeat**. You can feel a strong accent on this beat.

Other melodies begin on an unaccented note (or notes). An unaccented note at the beginning of a phrase is called an **upbeat** or a **pickup**. It can also be called an **anacrusis**.

If a melody begins on an upbeat, both the first measure and the last measure will be incomplete. The melody below is in 3/4 time. It begins on the third beat, which is a weak—or unaccented—beat. The first note of the melody is a quarter-note upbeat.

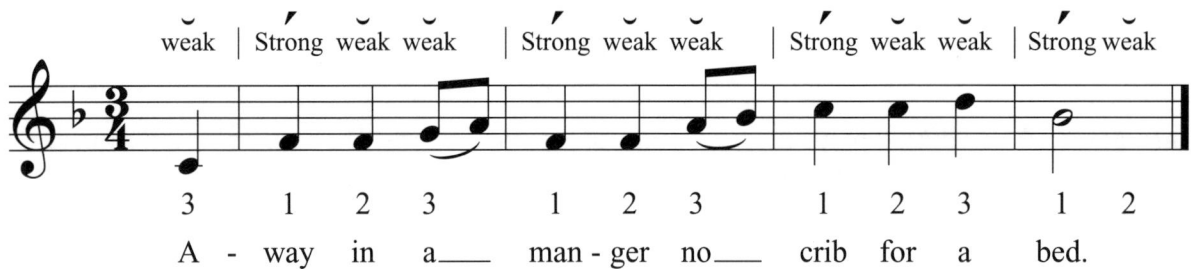

Take a close look at the first and last measures of this melody. Both measures are incomplete. The "missing" third beat of the last measure is equal to the upbeat that begins the melody. Together these two incomplete measures add up to one full measure. No rests are needed to complete these measures.

Remember that the *first complete* measure is m. 1.

The upbeat is not a complete measure.

Review of Scale Degree Names

Each note—or degree—of a scale has a **technical degree name**. Here are the three degree names you have learned so far. Find each one in the melody above.

Tonic: The first scale degree ($\hat{1}$) is called the **tonic**. A tonic note at the end of a melody gives the melody a "finished" sound.

Dominant: The fifth scale degree ($\hat{5}$) is called the **dominant**. A melody that begins with an upbeat often starts on the dominant. Many of these melodies begin with an ascending perfect 4th between the dominant ($\hat{5}$) and the tonic ($\hat{1}$).

Leading note: The seventh scale degree ($\hat{7}$) is called the **leading note**. Melodies often end with a step up from leading note ($\hat{7}$) to the tonic ($\hat{1}$).

Phrases and Cadences

A **phrase** is like a musical sentence. The notes in a phrase sound as if they belong together. Many end with a long note. Most melodies are made up of two or more phrases. Phrases are sometimes marked with a slur. Often, phrases are four measures long. Some phrases begin with an upbeat, as in the two melodies on the previous page.

All phrases end with a **cadence**. A cadence is like a punctuation mark in a sentence. Some cadences sound like endings, or periods. Others sound like pauses, or commas. For example, if you read a long sentence that has a comma part way through, you pause, but then continue. When you come to the period at the end of the sentence, you stop.

A melodic cadence usually involves the last two notes of the phrase. In most melodies, the last note of the phrase is longer than the others.

Imitation

The word "imitate" means "copy." Composers frequently use imitation when they create melodies. Play or sing Example 1 and listen for the imitation:

- m. 3 imitates m. 1
- m. 4 is different from m. 2

Measure 4 ends with the leading note rising to the tonic. These last two notes ($\hat{7}$–$\hat{1}$) create a melodic cadence.

Example 1

Play or sing Example 2, and listen for the imitation. This phrase starts on the dominant, as is often the case with a melody that begins with an upbeat.

- m. 3 imitates m. 1
- m. 4 is different from m. 2

Here again, the melody ends with the leading note rising to the tonic ($\hat{7}$–$\hat{1}$.) Notice that m. 4 has only three beats because of the quarter-note upbeat.

Example 2

Composing and Improvising

In previous levels of *Sound Advice*, you learned how to create your own melodies by writing a response to a two-measure melodic opening. On some of the Theory Worksheets, you were asked to sing responses to a given melodic opening. When you had a response you were satisfied with, you wrote it down. This process is called **composing**.

On some of your Ear-Training Worksheets, you were asked to sing or play a response to a given opening without hesitation. In other words, you made up the melody as you performed it. This process is called **improvising**. Always check the Ear-Training Answer Key for a possible response to the given opening.

Theory Worksheet

1 Draw a line to connect each group on the left with its corresponding note value on the right.

2 Fill in the blanks in the following sentences.

a) The dominant of B♭ major is _____.

b) The tonic of D major is _____.

c) The leading note of G major is _____.

d) The dominant of F major is _____.

e) The leading note of C major is _____.

3 Name the key of the following melody. Circle and label the tonic (T), the dominant (D), and the leading note (LN) each time they occur.

Key: _____

4 Play or sing the following melody, then answer the questions below.

Key:_____

a) Name the key.

b) Does this melody begin with an upbeat? _____

c) Write the measure numbers on the score. _____

d) How many measures are in this melody? _____

e) Does this melody sound finished? _____

f) Which measure imitates m. 1? _____

5 Sing or play the two-measure opening below, then improvise your own response. Your response should imitate the first measure and end on the tonic. Write down your response.

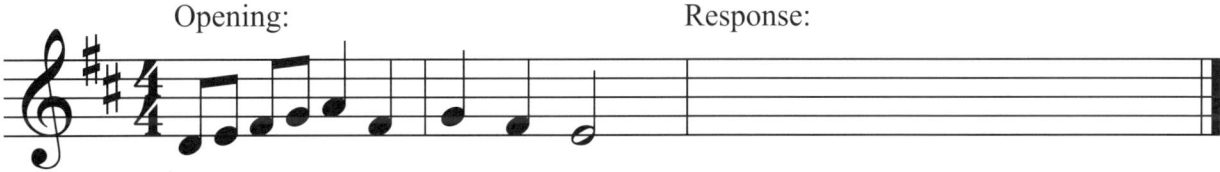

Key:_____

LESSON 7 Ear-Training Worksheet

1. Interval Identification: Identify the intervals you hear as ↗ min 2, maj 2, min 3, maj 3, P4, P5, maj 6, maj 7, or P8.

a)   b)   c)   d)   e)

f)   g)   h)   i)   j)

2. Sight Singing:

a) Pause the recording. Sing the following melody while you tap a steady quarter-note beat.

b) Turn to the answer key and sing along with the recording.

3. Editing: You will hear five pairs of notes. The first note of each pair will be played as written. Based on what you hear, write a sharp, flat, or natural to the *second* note. Each pair of notes will be played twice.

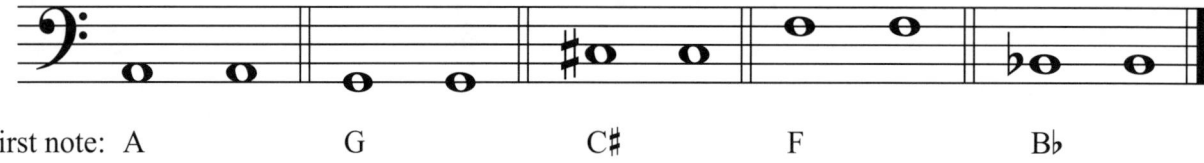

First note: A   G   C♯   F   B♭

4. Rhythm Clapback: Clap the *rhythm* of the melody you hear from memory. Record the number of times you listened.

LESSON 7
Ear-Training Worksheet

5 **Melodic Dictation:** Add the missing notes under the bracket. The melody will be played twice.

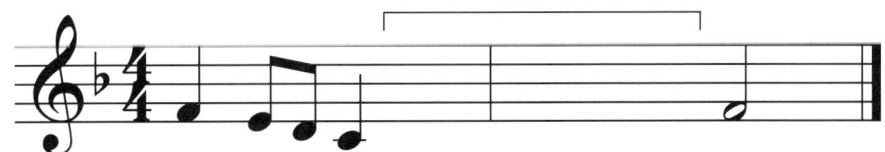

6 **Melodic Improvisation:** You will hear a two-measure opening.
  a) Improvise a two-measure response.
  b) Write your response on the staff below. Your melody should end on the tonic.

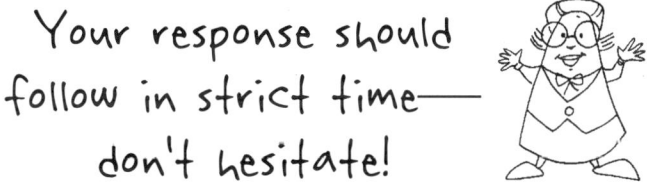

Your response should follow in strict time— don't hesitate!

Learning Guide

Major and Minor 2nds: A Shortcut

Remember this shortcut for identifying the quality (major or minor) of a 2nd without referring to the scale and key signature of the lower note.

Major 2nds are always whole steps (W). Minor 2nds are always half steps ($\frac{1}{2}$).

maj 2 = W   min 2 = $\frac{1}{2}$

Major and Minor 3rds: A Shortcut

Here is the shortcut you can use to identify the quality (major or minor) of a 3rd without referring to the scale and key signature of the lower note.

Major 3rds are made up of two whole steps: think of "W + W."   Minor 3rds are made up of a whole step plus a half step: think of "W + $\frac{1}{2}$" or "$\frac{1}{2}$ + W."

maj 3 = W + W   min 3 = W + $\frac{1}{2}$

Count the steps in the 2nds and 3rds below. Remember that the minor 3rds can be "W + $\frac{1}{2}$" or "$\frac{1}{2}$ + W."

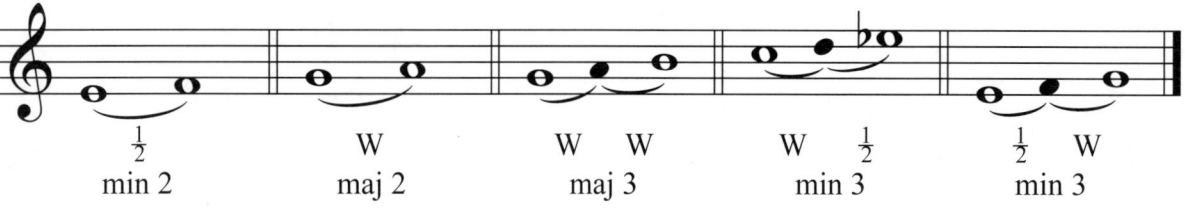

Learning Guide 8

Enharmonic Notes and Intervals

You have learned that a pitch can have at least two different spellings. Two notes that are spelled differently but represent the same key on the keyboard (for example, G♯ and A♭) are called **enharmonic equivalents**.

Intervals can also have different spellings. For example E–F♯ is a whole step. It can also be called a major 2nd if the two notes have two *consecutive* letter names. However, if you change the top note from F♯ to G♭ (its enharmonic equivalent), the interval becomes a 3rd. Although the sound is the same, you can't call E–G♭ a major 2nd because it is spelled as a 3rd. These two intervals are shown on the keyboard below.

This is a whole step.
It also is a maj 2nd.

This is a whole step.
It is NOT a maj 2nd.

These sound the same, but the second example does not have two consecutive letter names.

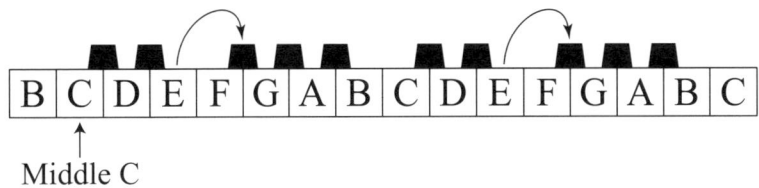

↑
Middle C

The same applies to half steps. For example, the half step E–F can also be called a minor 2nd if the two notes have *consecutive* letter names. If you change the top note from F to E♯ (its enharmonic equivalent), the interval is no longer a 2nd, even though the sound is the same, because one letter name is used.

This is a half step.
It is also a min 2nd.

This is a half step.
It is NOT a min 2nd.

Same thing here! The second example does not have two consecutive letter names.

Mad Music Game: Name the 3rds

Beginning with this lesson, you can play Mad Music as an interval naming game. The Mad Music Interval Chart is on p. 137. Your goal is to accurately name all the major and minor 3rds on the chart in two minutes or less. Try to achieve this goal before you begin Lesson 13.

If you have not yet achieved the Mad Music major key signature goal, continue working on it, but start the new interval game as well.

LESSON 8 Theory Worksheet

1   a) Identify the following pairs of notes as whole steps (W) or half steps ($\frac{1}{2}$) by circling the W or $\frac{1}{2}$ above the staff. You may use the keyboard to help you.
    b) Name each interval as a major or minor 2nd. The first one has been done for you.

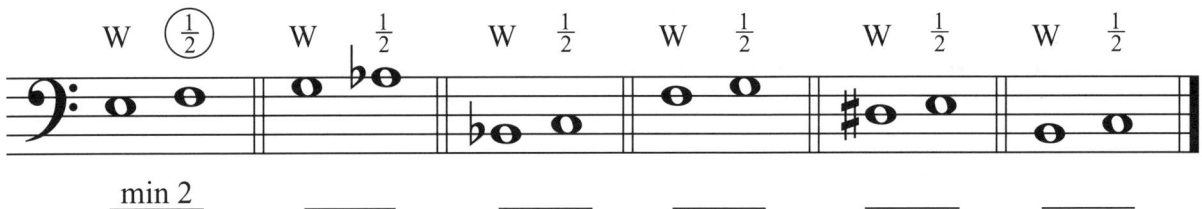

2   a) Identify the following pairs of notes as W+W or W+$\frac{1}{2}$ by circling your answer above the staff.
    b) Name each interval as a major 3rd or a minor 3rd. The first one has been done for you.

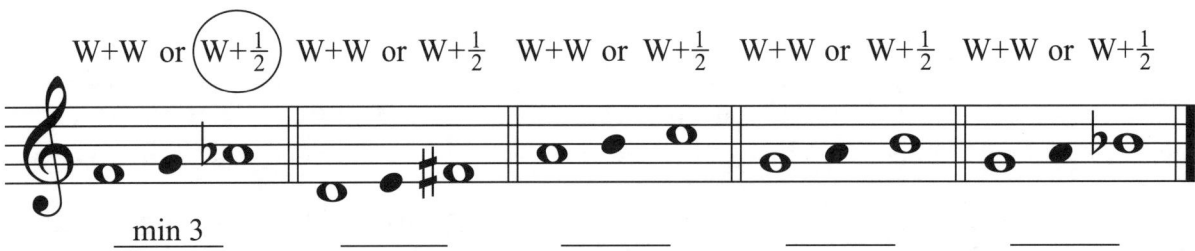

3   Draw a line from each interval in the upper staff to its enharmonic equivalent in the lower staff. The first one has been done for you.

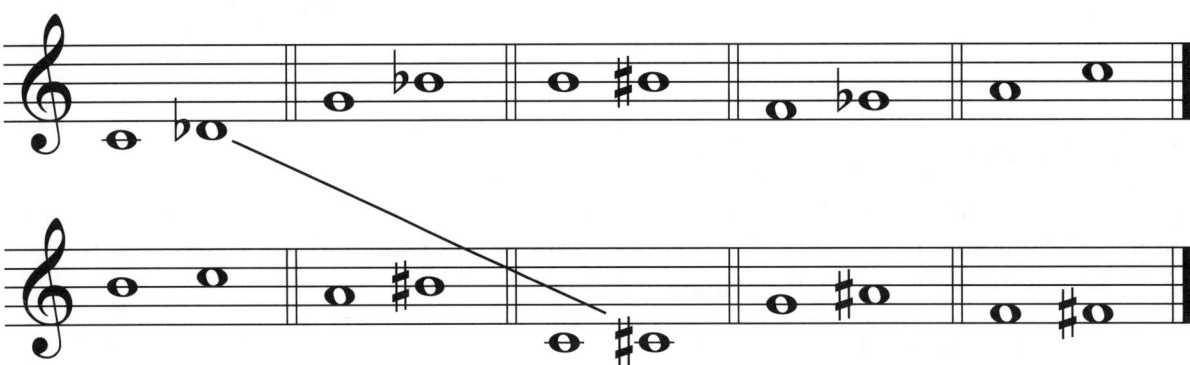

4   Mad Music Scores   ☐ ☐ ☐

Ear-Training Worksheet

LESSON 8

 1 **Sight Singing:**

a) Pause the recording. Sing the following melody while you tap a steady quarter-note beat.

b) Turn to the answer key and sing along with the recording.

 2 **Interval Identification:** Identify the intervals you hear as ↗ min 2, maj 2, min 3, maj 3, P4, P5, maj 6, maj 7, or P8.

a)   b)   c)   d)   e)

f)   g)   h)   i)   j)

 3 **Editing:** The following intervals are written as major 2nds or major 3rds. If you hear a major interval on the recording, leave the interval as written. If you hear a minor interval, add the appropriate accidental to the upper note.

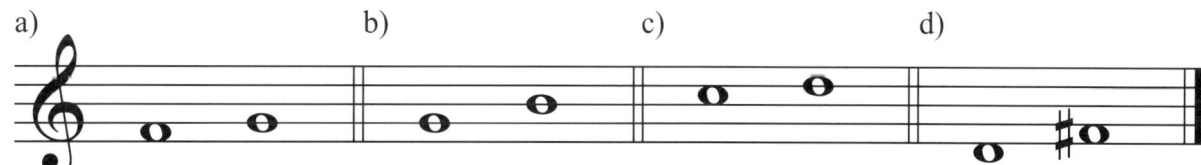

 4 **Melodic Dictation:** Add the missing notes under the bracket. The melody will be played twice.

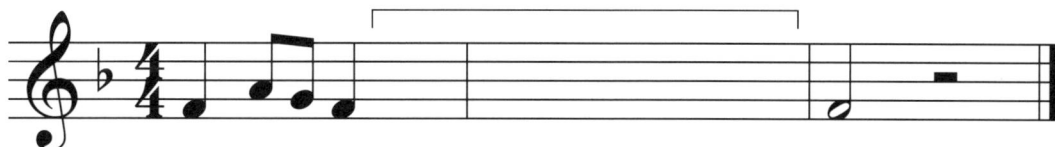

 5 **Rhythmic Dictation:** Write the rhythmic pattern you hear in the space below. Listen as many times as you need. The rhythm is in 3/4 time.

Write it down as you hear it!

Learning Guide

Major Triads

A **chord** consists of three or more pitches that sound together. A **triad** is a three-note chord. A **major triad** consists of the first, third, and fifth notes of a major scale ($\hat{1}$–$\hat{3}$–$\hat{5}$).

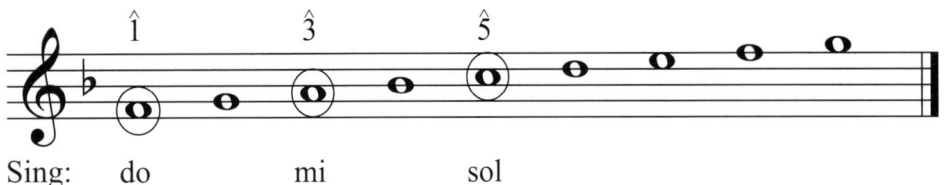

Sing: do   mi   sol

The notes of a triad can be played separately (broken) or together (solid or blocked).
The bottom note of a triad is called the **root**. The middle note is called the **third**, and the top note is called the **fifth**.

F major triad
broken

F major triad
solid (blocked)

Minor Triads

When the middle note (the third) of a major triad is lowered a half step, the chord becomes a **minor triad**.

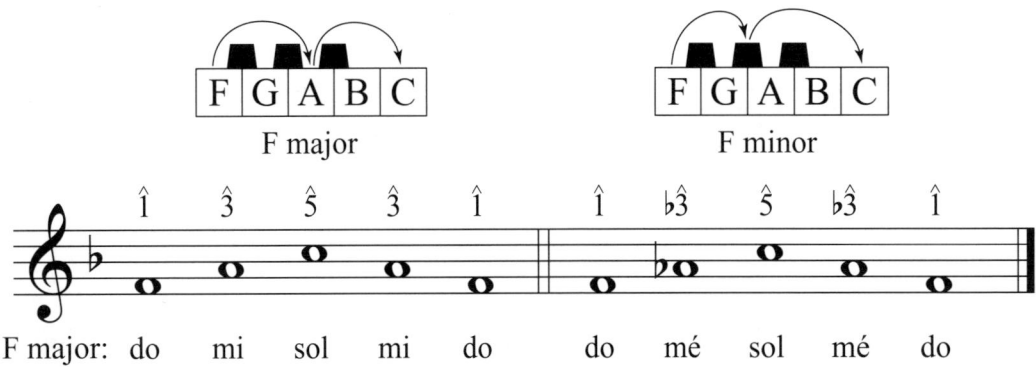

F major: do   mi   sol   mi   do   do   mé   sol   mé   do

To turn a major triad into a minor triad, you will need an accidental to lower the third. If the third of the triad does not have an accidental, add a flat sign to lower it. If the third has a sharp, add a natural sign to lower it.

Play the following major and minor triads. Listen to the contrast in sound between each pair.

C maj C min   G maj G min   D maj D min   F maj F min   B♭ maj B♭ min

Lesson 9 Learning Guide   Sound Advice Level 4

Learning Guide — Lesson 9

A Closer Look at Triads

The interval between the root and the third is a 3rd. The interval between the root and the fifth is a 5th. You can also see that major and minor triads are made up of two 3rds stacked one on top of the other.

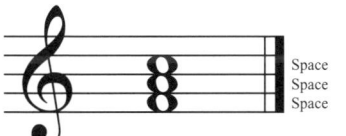
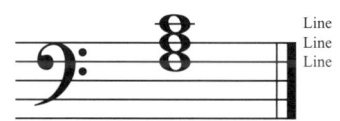

Triads look like snowmen. A stack of 3rds!

Major triads have a major 3rd on the bottom and a minor 3rd on top.

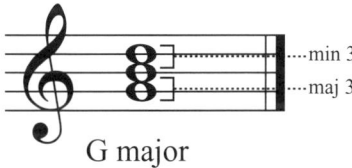

G major

Minor triads have a minor 3rd on the bottom and a major 3rd on the top.

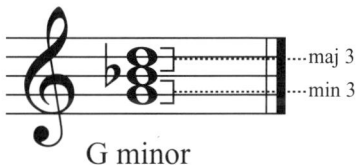

G minor

Arpeggios

You can create a broken four-note chord, or **arpeggio**, by doubling the root of a triad an octave above.

Play the following major and minor arpeggios. The major arpeggio is a one-octave arpeggio. The minor arpeggio is a two-octave arpeggio.

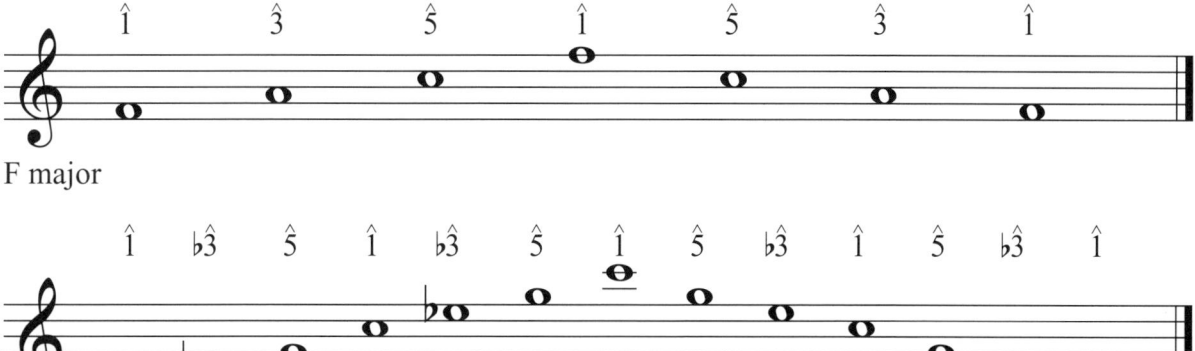

F major

C minor

Sound Advice Level 4

LESSON 9 Learning Guide

The Sound of Descending Intervals: min 3, P5, P8

So far, we have been reviewing the sound of the ascending intervals. Now it's time to look at descending intervals.

The descending minor 3rd, perfect 5th, and perfect 8ve can be found between notes of a major triad or a major arpeggio.

Play or sing these three examples.

min 3

P5

P8

You can also memorize the sound of these intervals by relating them to familiar melodies. The Song Clue Chart on p. 134 lists several clues for each interval.

TIP: If you ever have difficulty identifying the sound of an interval, you may find it helpful to sing the two notes back to yourself in the opposite order. Think of this as "flipping" the interval.

For example, if you hear this:

sing this:

You can flip them!

Turn to the Song Clue Chart on p. 134 and put a ✔ beside the descending minor 3rd (min 3), perfect 5th (P5), and perfect 8ve (P8).

Theory Worksheet

LESSON 9

1 a) Write a B♭ major scale in whole notes, ascending only. Use a key signature.

b) Circle the notes that make a B♭ major triad.

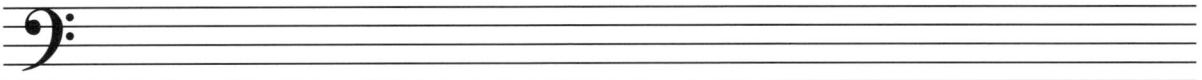

2 Write the following solid triads on the staff below, using accidentals.

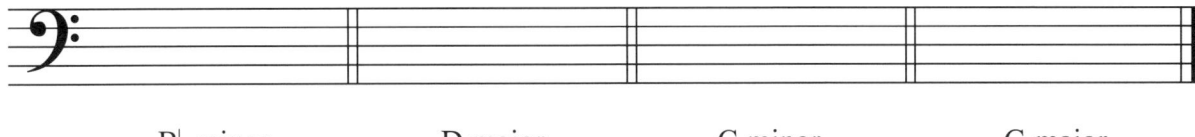

B♭ minor   D major   C minor   G major

3 Write a D major two-octave arpeggio in whole notes, ascending and descending. Use a key signature.

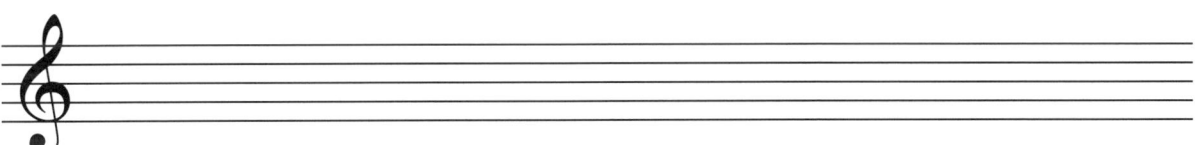

4 The following intervals are all half steps. Circle the ones that are minor 2nds.

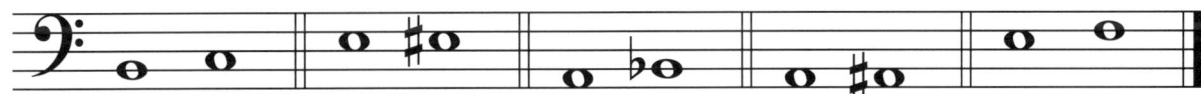

5 For each interval, answer the questions, then write the full name of the interval in the space provided.

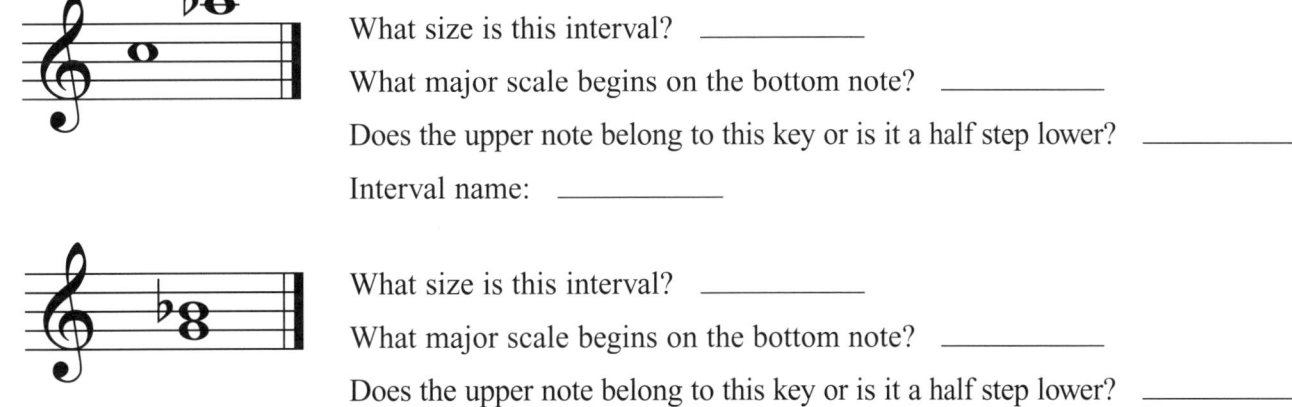

What size is this interval? _____

What major scale begins on the bottom note? _____

Does the upper note belong to this key or is it a half step lower? _____

Interval name: _____

What size is this interval? _____

What major scale begins on the bottom note? _____

Does the upper note belong to this key or is it a half step lower? _____

Interval name: _____

6 Mad Music Scores ☐ ☐ ☐

LESSON 9 — Ear-Training Worksheet

 1 **Interval Identification:** Identify the intervals you hear as ↗ min 2, maj 2, min 3, maj 3, P4, P5, maj6, maj 7, P8, ↘ min 3, P5, or P8.

a)   b)   c)   d)   e)

f)   g)   h)   i)   j)

 2 **Triad Identification:** Identify the triads you hear as major or minor. Each triad will be played twice: once in solid form and once in broken form.

a)   b)   c)   d)   e)

 3 **Editing:** The following triads are written as major triads. If you hear a major triad on the recording, leave the triad as written. If you hear a minor triad, add the appropriate accidental to the middle note.

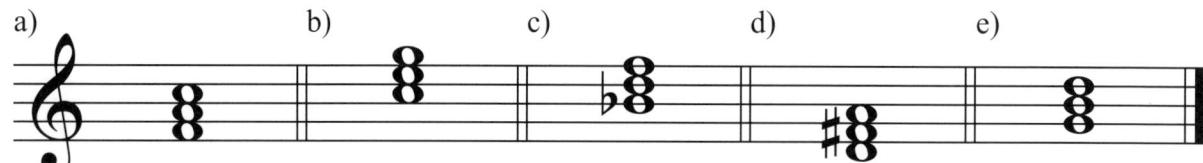

 4 **Triads:** You will hear a major triad followed by the root, the third, or the fifth of the triad. Write the note you hear on the staff beside the triad.

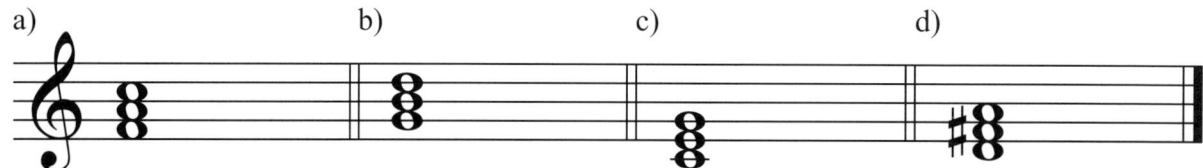

 5 **Sight Singing:**
 a) Pause the recording. Sing the following melody while you tap a steady quarter-note beat.
 b) Turn to the answer key and sing along with the recording.

Learning Guide

The Natural Minor Scale

Play the scale below.

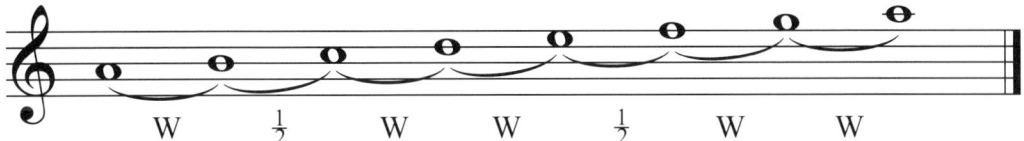

This scale begins on A: it is an A **natural minor scale**. This scale—like the C major scale—does not have any sharps or flats. The C major scale and the A natural minor scale use the same notes. However, A natural minor sounds different from C major because it begins on A and it has a different order of whole steps and half steps.

Relative Major and Minor Scales

Every major scale is related to a minor scale, its **relative minor**. The relative natural minor scale shares the same key signature and the same notes with its relative major.

The following example will help you hear how a natural minor scale relates to its relative major scale. Play or sing it using these three steps.

1) Play or sing up the major scale and pause on $\hat{1}$ (do).
2) Sing down $\hat{1}$–$\hat{7}$–$\hat{6}$ (do–ti–la). Pause on $\hat{6}$ (la).
3) When you are comfortably rooted on $\hat{6}$ (la), sing all the way up from $\hat{6}$ to $\hat{6}$ (la to la). (You will have to sing "in your head" when the notes move out of your vocal range.)

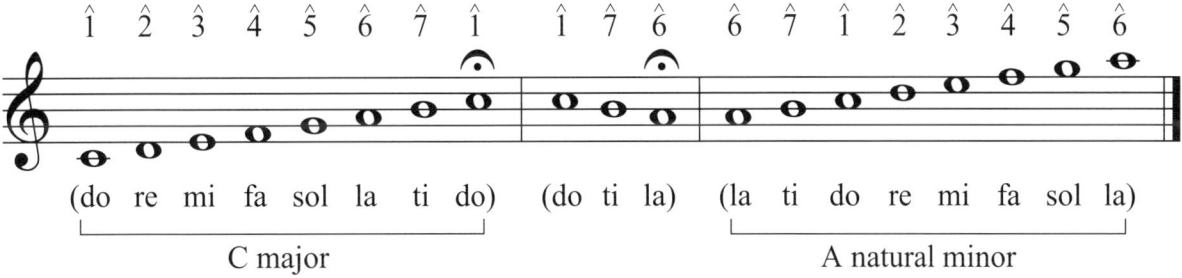

The A natural minor scale starts on the sixth degree of C major, its relative major scale. However, A is the tonic note: it is numbered $\hat{1}$ as the first scale degree.

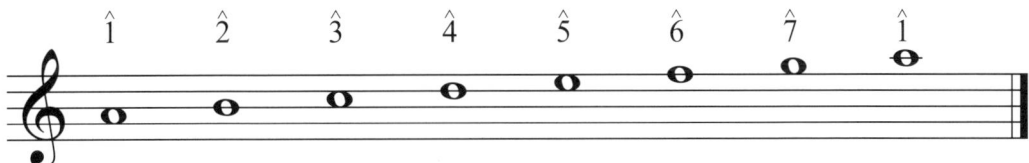

Sight Singing in Minor Keys

If you use movable do syllables for sight singing, you can choose one of two syllable patterns for minor keys. In one pattern, the first scale degree is la. In the other pattern, the first scale degree is do. Ask your teacher which pattern you should use. (For more information on sight-singing syllables, see the Appendix on pp. 167–168.)

On your recording, all the examples in minor keys will be played on the piano. This way you can check your accuracy using the syllables that work best for you.

LESSON 10 Theory Worksheet

1 Write the following key signatures on the grand staff.

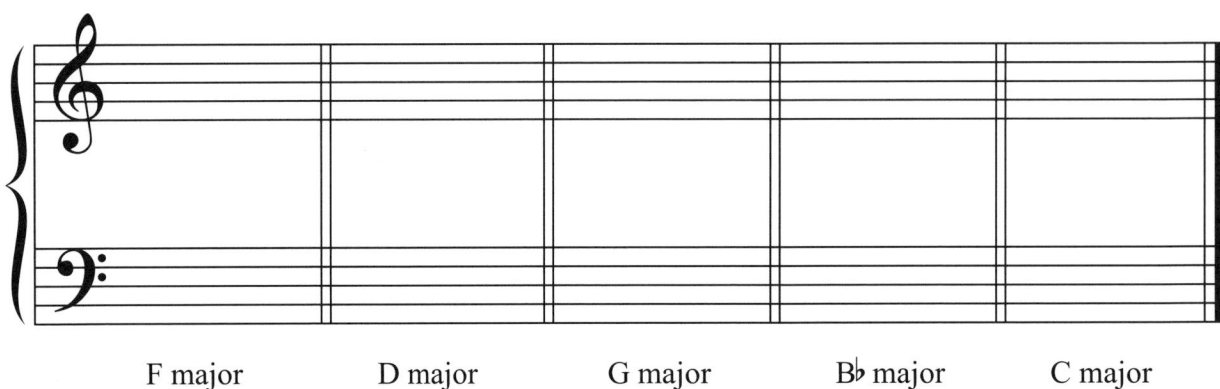

F major   D major   G major   B♭ major   C major

2 a) Identify the following pairs of notes as either W+W or W+½ by circling the correct answer.

b) Name each interval as a maj 3 or a min 3.

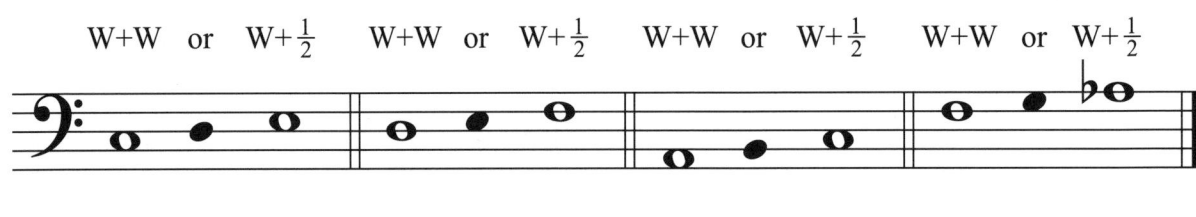

3 Write an ascending A natural minor scale in whole notes. Mark the whole steps and half steps.

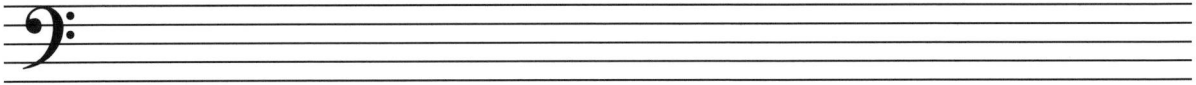

4 Write the following triads in solid (blocked) form. Use key signatures.

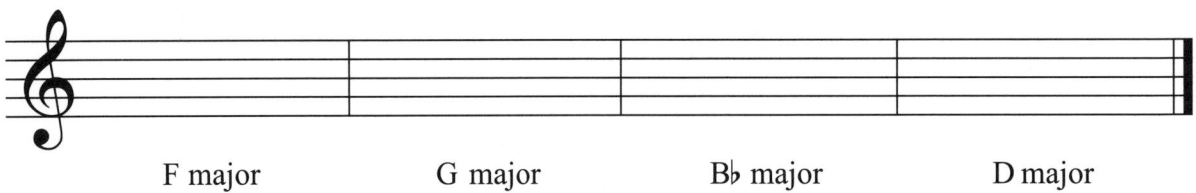

F major   G major   B♭ major   D major

5 The following intervals are all whole steps. Circle the ones that are major 2nds.

6 Mad Music Scores ☐ ☐ ☐

56   Lesson 10 Theory Worksheet   Sound Advice Level 4

LESSON 10

Ear-Training Worksheet

 1 **Interval Identification:** Identify the intervals you hear as ↗ min 2, maj 2, min 3, maj 3, P4, P5, maj 6, maj 7, P8, ↘ min 3, P5, or P8.

a)   b)   c)   d)   e)

f)   g)   h)   i)   j)

 2 **Sight Singing:**
a) Pause the recording. Sing an A natural minor scale, ascending and descending.

b) Turn to the answer key and sing along with the recording.

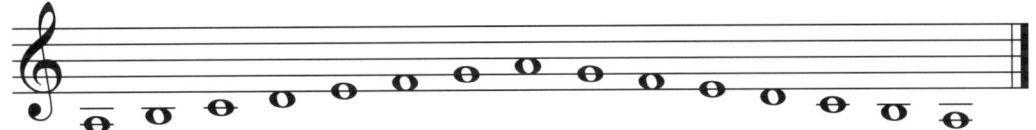

 3 **Sight Singing:**
a) Pause the recording. Sing the following melody while you tap a steady quarter-note beat.

b) Turn to the answer key and sing along with the recording.

 4 **Scale Identification:** Identify the scales you hear as natural minor (nm) or major (maj).

a)   b)   c)   d)

 5 **Triads:** You will hear a minor triad followed by the root, the third, or the fifth of the triad. Write the note that you hear on the staff beside the triad.

a)   b)   c)   d)

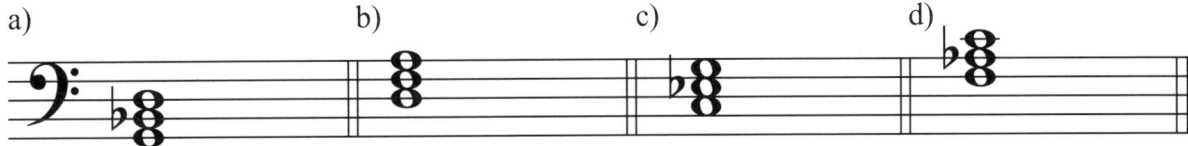

 6 **Melodic Improvisation:** You will hear a two-measure opening.
a) Improvise a two-measure response.

b) Write your response on the staff below. Your melody should end on the tonic.

Sound Advice Level 4   Lesson 10 Ear-Training Worksheet   57

Learning Guide

Two New Minor Scales: E Minor and B Minor

The E natural minor scale shares the same key signature and uses the same notes as the G major scale.

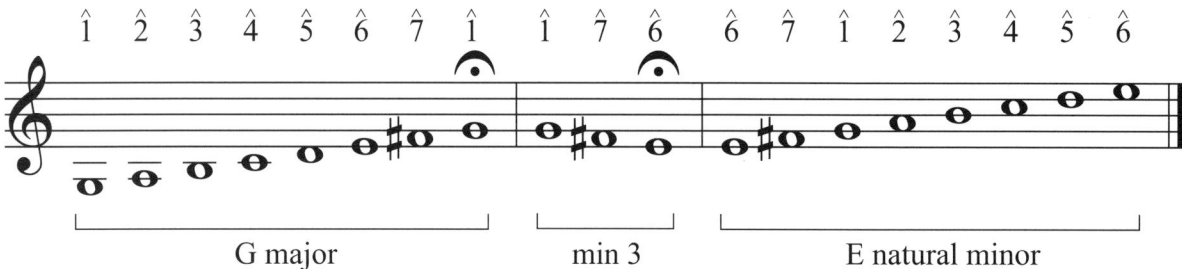

The B natural minor scale shares the same key signature and uses the same notes as the D major scale.

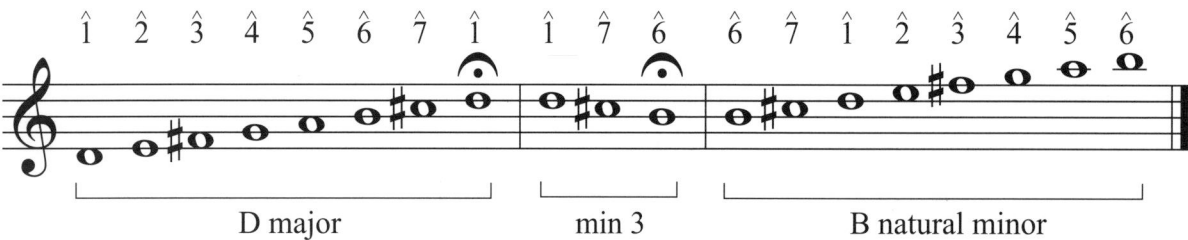

Major and Minor Relatives

Take a second look at the two scales above. Notice that the last three notes ($\hat{6}-\hat{7}-\hat{1}$) of the major scales are the same as the first three notes ($\hat{1}-\hat{2}-\hat{3}$) of the relative minor scales.

To find a relative minor scale, play the first three notes of the descending major scale ($\hat{1}-\hat{7}-\hat{6}$) and stop on $\hat{6}$. This note is $\hat{1}$ of the relative minor scale. Here are three examples.

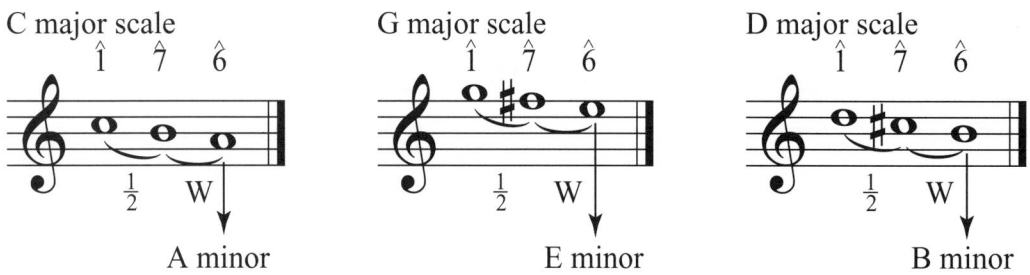

In a major scale, the descending interval from $\hat{1}$ down to $\hat{6}$ is a minor 3rd (a half step followed by a whole step).

Learning Guide

Lesson 11

How to Identify Relative Major and Minor Scales

If you know the major scale and are looking for the relative minor scale, go *down* a minor 3rd ($\frac{1}{2}$+W). That note is the tonic ($\hat{1}$) of the relative minor scale.

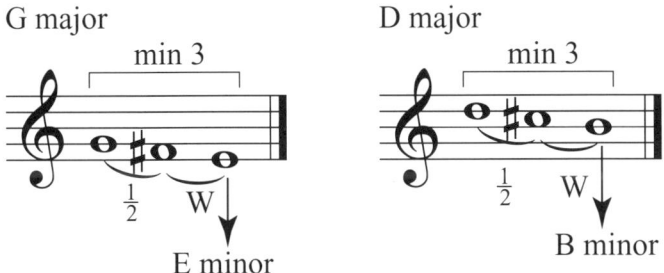

If you know the minor scale and are looking for the relative major scale, go *up* a minor 3rd (W+$\frac{1}{2}$). That note is the tonic ($\hat{1}$) of the relative major scale.

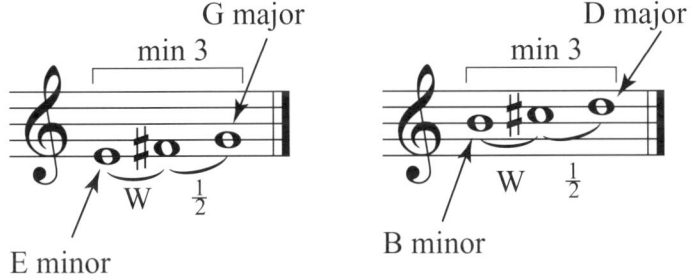

TIP: If you forget which direction to go, think about baseball. As you can see in the picture below, the major league player is stepping *down* to get to the minor league field. The minor league player is stepping *up* to get to the major league field.

Sound Advice Level 4   Lesson 11 Learning Guide

LESSON 11 Theory Worksheet

1 Each of the following notes is $\hat{1}$ of a minor key. Find the relative major by writing a minor 3rd (W+$\frac{1}{2}$) *above* the given note.

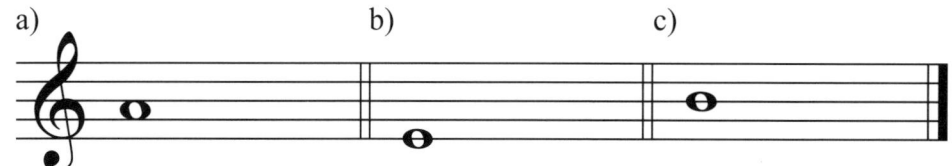

2 Each of the following notes is $\hat{1}$ of a major key. Find the relative minor by writing the note that is a minor 3rd ($\frac{1}{2}$+W) *below* the given note.

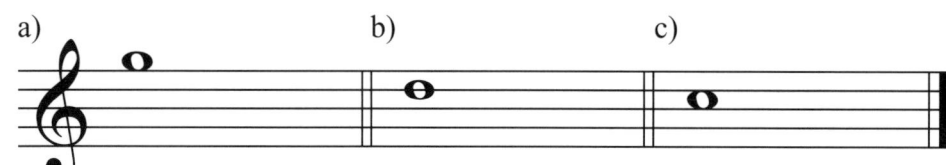

Hint: You can think of a descending major scale!

3 Write an ascending E natural minor scale in whole notes. Use accidentals.

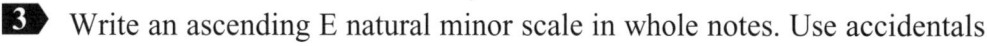

4 Write an ascending B natural minor scale in whole notes. Use accidentals.

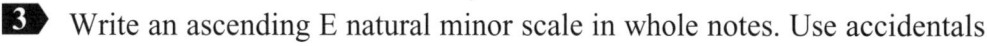

5 Circle the quarter-note beats in the following examples, then add time signatures.

a)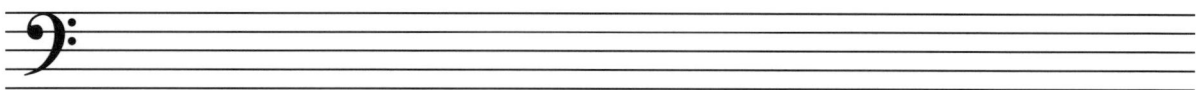

b)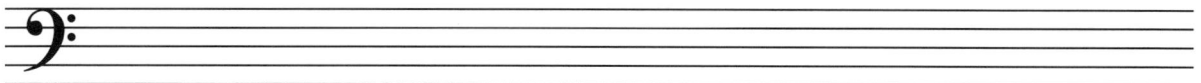

6 One-Minute Rhythm Jumble: Record the number of days you practiced.

7 Mad Music Scores

Ear-Training Worksheet

LESSON 11

1. Interval Identification: Identify the intervals you hear as ↗ min 2, maj 2, min 3, maj 3, P4, P5, maj 6, maj 7, P8, ↘ min 3, P5, or P8.

a)   b)   c)   d)   e)

f)   g)   h)   i)   j)

2. Scale Identification: Identify the scales you hear as either major or minor.

a)   b)   c)   d)   e)

3. Sight Singing:
a) Pause the recording. Sing the E natural minor scale, ascending and descending.
b) Turn to the answer key and sing along with the recording.

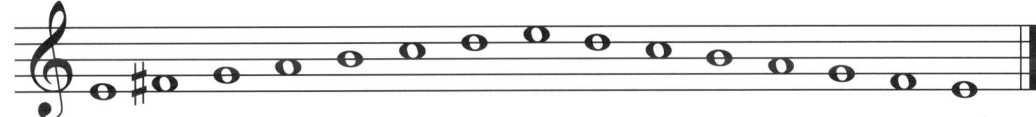

4. Sight Singing:
a) Pause the recording. Sing the following melody while you tap a steady quarter-note beat.
b) Turn to the answer key and sing along with the recording.

Ma-jor league to mi-nor league, woe is me!   Half step, whole step, mi-nor key!

5. Sight Singing:
a) Pause the recording. Sing the following melody while you tap a steady quarter-note beat.
b) Turn to the answer key and sing along with the recording.

Mi-nor league to ma-jor league, good for me!   Whole step, half step, ma-jor key!

Learning Guide

Minor Key Signatures with Sharps

To identify minor key signatures with sharps, you can use the same shortcut you learned for major key signatures. The only difference is that you start on A. For example, the key of A minor has no sharps. The key signature of E minor (which is a 5th higher) has one sharp. The key signature of B minor has two sharps, and so on.

So far you have learned two minor keys with sharp key signatures. The placement and order of the sharps is the same as it is for the relative major keys: the sharps go up by 5ths.

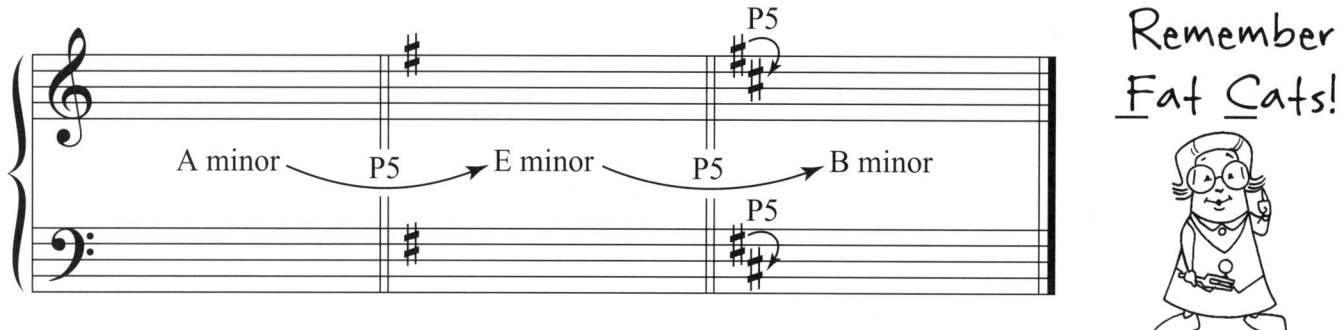

Remember Fat Cats!

Writing Minor Scales with a Key Signature

It is easy to write a natural minor scale if you know the key signature. If you forget the key signature, count up a minor 3rd (W+$\frac{1}{2}$) to find the key signature of the relative major.

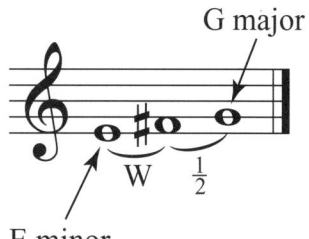

E minor

When you write a natural minor scale with a key signature, follow these five steps. Try them with an E natural minor scale in whole notes, ascending and descending:

1) Identify the relative major key. (G major)
2) Write the major key signature on the staff. (1 sharp)
3) Write the first note of the scale. (E)
4) Write the rest of the scale, as instructed. (whole notes, ascending and descending)
5) Put a double bar line at the end.

Your scale should look like this:

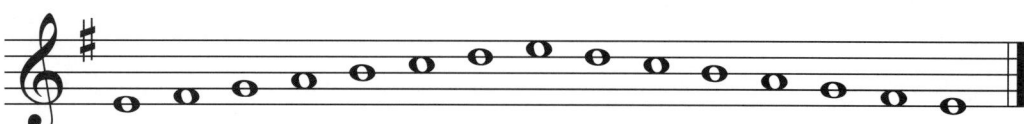

E natural minor

Theory Worksheet — LESSON 12

1 Each of the following notes is $\hat{1}$ of a minor key. Find the relative major by writing a minor 3rd (W+$\frac{1}{2}$) *above* the given note.

a)   b)   c)

2 Each of the following notes is $\hat{1}$ of a major key. Find the relative minor by writing a minor 3rd ($\frac{1}{2}$+W) *below* the given note.

a)   b)   c)

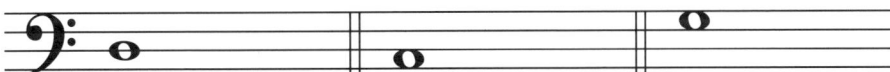

Hint: You can think of a descending major scale!

3 Write the following key signatures on the grand staff below.

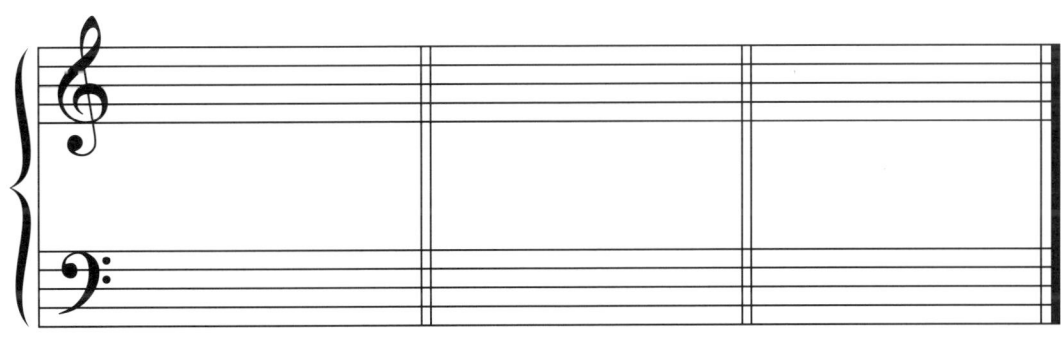

A minor   E minor   B minor

4 Write a B natural minor scale in whole notes, ascending and descending. Use a key signature.

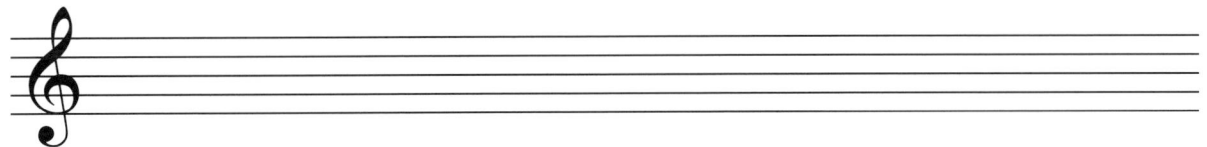

5 Write an E natural minor scale in whole notes, descending only. Use a key signature.

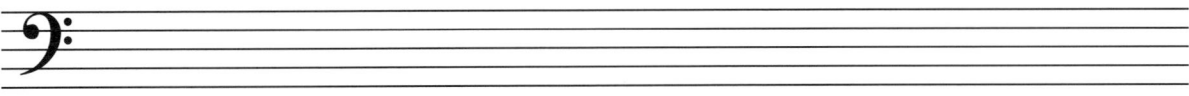

Sound Advice Level 4   Lesson 12 Theory Worksheet   63

LESSON 12 Theory Worksheet

6 Draw a line from each group of notes and rests on the left to its corresponding note value on the right.

   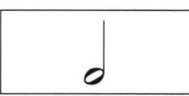

7 Draw a line from each group on the left to its corresponding note value on the right.

8 Circle the quarter-note beats. Add bar lines according to the time signature.

a)

b)

LESSON 12
Ear-Training Worksheet

1 **Interval Identification:** Identify the intervals you hear as ↗ min 2, maj 2, min 3, maj 3, P4, P5, maj 6, maj 7, P8, ↘ min 3, P5, or P8.

a)   b)   c)   d)   e)

f)   g)   h)   i)   j)

2 **Scale Identification:** Identify the scales you hear as either major or minor.

a)   b)   c)   d)   e)

3 **Sight Singing:**
a) Pause the recording. Sing a B natural minor scale, ascending and descending.
b) Turn to the answer key and sing along with the recording.

4 **Rhythmic Reading:**
a) Pause the recording. Sing the following rhythmic pattern while you tap a steady quarter-note beat.
b) Turn to the answer key and sing along with the recording.

5 **Rhythmic Identification:** Identify the correct notation for the rhythmic pattern you hear. Each pattern will be played twice.

6 **Melody Singback/Playback:** Sing the melody you hear from memory, then play it on your instrument. The melody is in the key of B minor, in 4/4 time.

Learning Guide

Two New Minor Scales: D Minor and G Minor

The D natural minor scale shares the same key signature and uses the same notes as the F major scale.

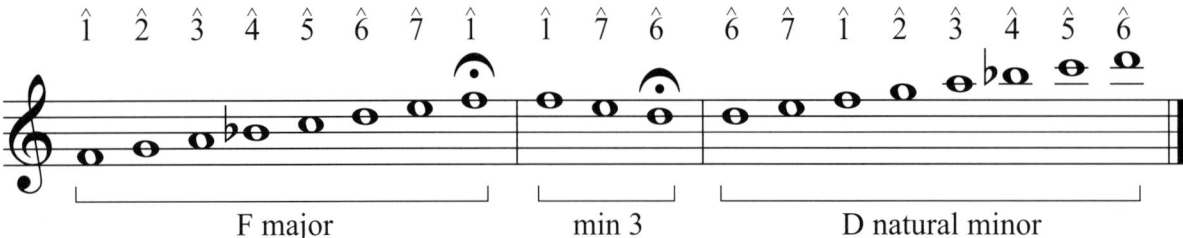

The G minor scale shares the same key signature and uses the same notes as the Bb major scale.

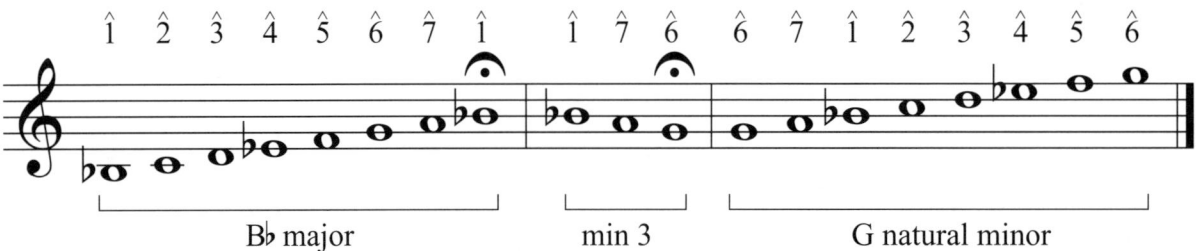

Minor Key Signatures with Flats

To identify the minor key signatures with flats, you can use the same shortcut you learned for major key signatures. The only difference is that you start on A. For example, the key of A minor has no flats. The key signature of D minor (which is a 4th higher) has one flat. The key signature of G minor has two flats, and so on.

So far you have learned two minor keys with flat key signatures. The placement and order of the flats is the same as it is for the relative major keys: the flats go up by 4ths.

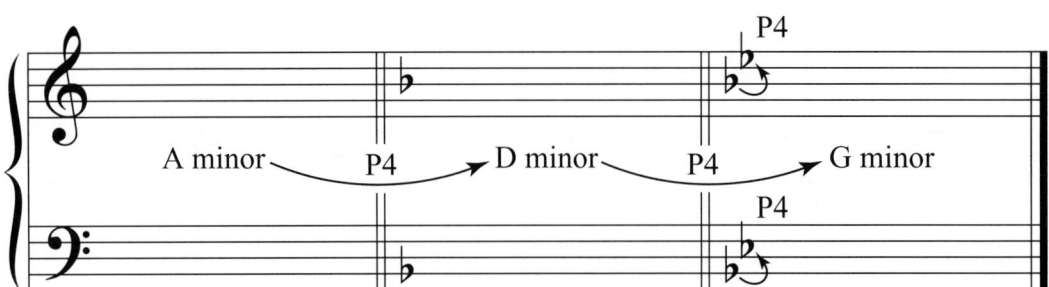

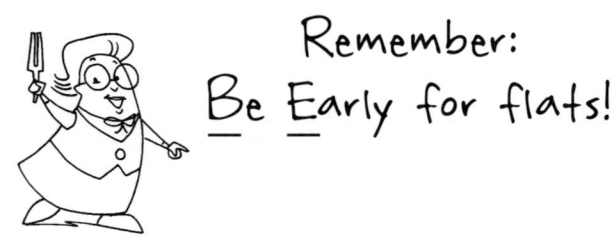

Remember: **B**e **E**arly for flats!

Learning Guide

Lesson 13

Writing Minor Scales with Accidentals

When you write a natural minor scale using accidentals instead of a key signature, follow these five steps. Try them with a G natural minor scale in whole notes, ascending and descending:

1) Identify the relative major. (B♭ major)
2) Write the sharps or flats of the key signature above the staff. (B♭, E♭)
3) Write the notes of the minor scale on the staff, as instructed. (Whole notes, ascending and descending)
4) Cross out each sharp or flat written above the staff as you add the accidentals to the notes. (Remember to write the accidentals in front of the notes, on the same space or line as the noteheads.)
5) If the scale is ascending and descending, do not repeat the accidentals on the way down unless there is a bar line halfway through the scale.

Your scale should look like this:

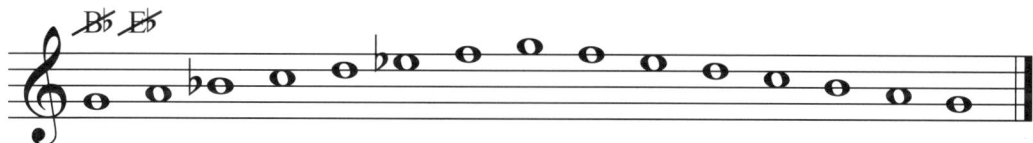

G natural minor

Mad Music Game: Minor Key Signatures

Beginning with this lesson, you can play Mad Music as a minor key signature game. The Mad Music Key Signature Chart is on p. 136. Your goal is to accurately name all the minor keys on the chart in twenty seconds or less.

If you have not yet achieved one or both of the previous Mad Music goals, continue working on them, but start the new minor key signature game as well. Once you achieve all three goals, you will have earned the status of Mad Music Expert, and will be awarded a Certificate of Achievement (see the inside back cover).

However, you should continue to play the Mad Music key signatures and major and minor 3rds games even after you become a Mad Music Expert.

LESSON 13 Theory Worksheet

1. Each of the following notes is $\hat{1}$ of a minor key. Find the relative major by writing a minor 3rd (W+$\frac{1}{2}$) above the given notes.

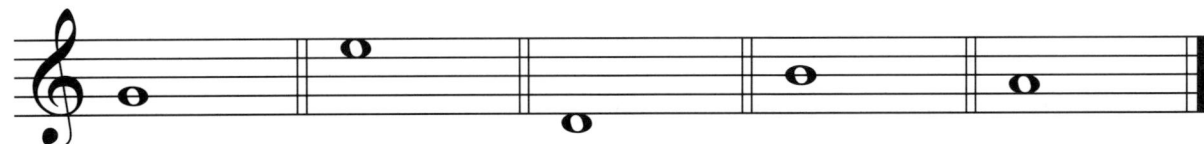

2. Each of the following notes is $\hat{1}$ of a major key. Find the relative minor by writing a minor 3rd ($\frac{1}{2}$+W) below the given notes.

3. Write the following key signatures on the grand staff below.

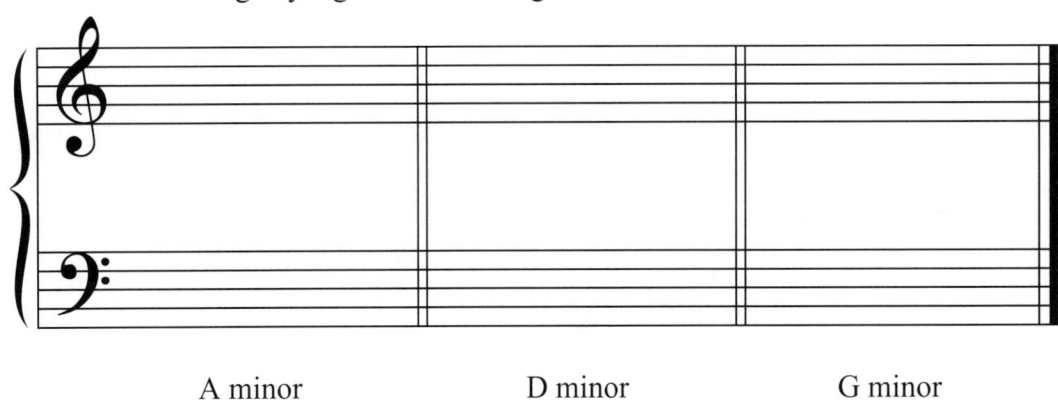

A minor   D minor   G minor

4. Write a G natural minor scale in whole notes, ascending and descending. Use accidentals.

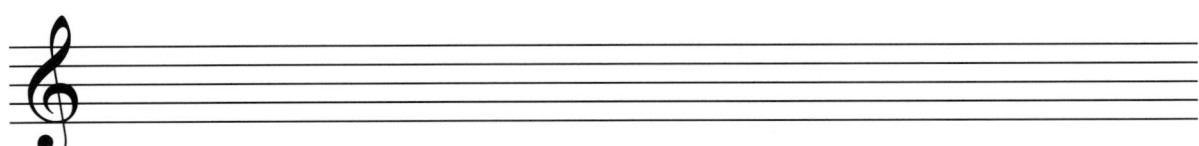

5. Write a D natural minor scale in whole notes, ascending only. Use accidentals.

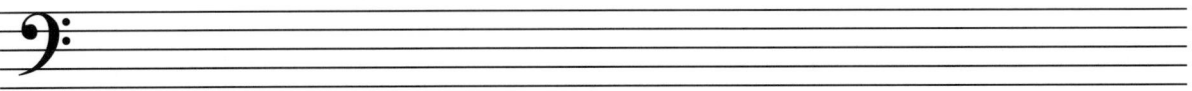

Theory Worksheet — LESSON 13

6 For each interval below, answer the questions, then name the interval (size and quality) on the line provided.

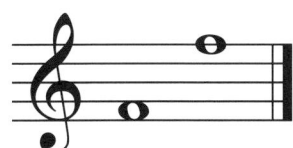

What size is this interval? _____

What major scale begins on the bottom note? _____

Does the upper note belong to this key or is it a half step lower? _____

Interval name: _____

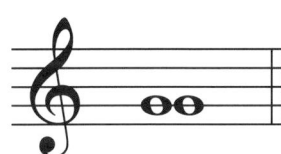

What size is this interval? _____

What major scale begins on the bottom note? _____

Does the upper note belong to this key or is it a half step lower? _____

Interval name: _____

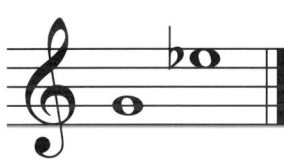

What size is this interval? _____

What major scale begins on the bottom note? _____

Does the upper note belong to this key or is it a half step lower? _____

Interval name: _____

What size is this interval? _____

What major scale begins on the bottom note? _____

Does the upper note belong to this key or is it a half step lower? _____

Interval name: _____

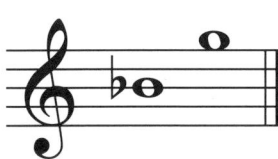

What size is this interval? _____

What major scale begins on the bottom note? _____

Does the upper note belong to this key or is it a half step lower? _____

Interval name: _____

7 Mad Music Scores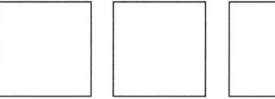

LESSON 13 — Ear-Training Worksheet

 1 **Interval Identification:** You will hear five intervals. The first note of each interval is given below. Name the interval and write the second note. Each interval will be played twice.

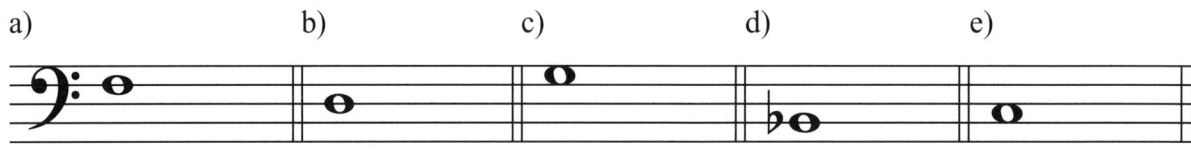

 2 **Rhythmic Dictation:**
a) Clap the *rhythm* of the melody you hear from memory.
b) Write it in the space below. The rhythm is in 2/4 time.

 3 **Melodic Dictation:** Add the missing notes under the bracket. The melody will be played twice.

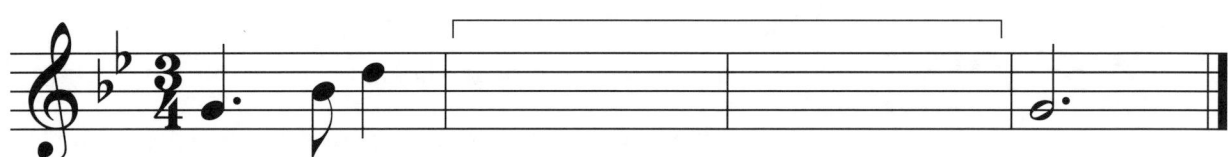

 4 **Melodic Improvisation:** You will hear a two-measure opening.
a) Improvise a two-measure response.
b) Write your response on the staff below. Your melody should end on the tonic.

 5 **Editing:**
a) Add ties where you hear them in the following rhythmic pattern. Listen as many times as you need.
b) Sing the edited rhythmic pattern while you tap a steady quarter-note beat.

 Add ties!

A Closer Look at Dotted Notes

A dot increases the length of a note by one half of its original value, as shown in the following examples.

New Rhythmic Unit

This new rhythmic unit is equal to a quarter note. The dotted eighth note equals three sixteenth notes.

The sixteenth note completes the quarter-note beat.

Sing the following rhythmic units:

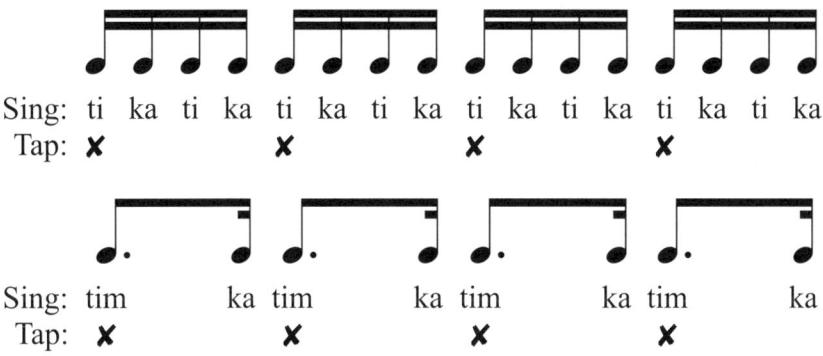

Sing: ti ka ti ka ti ka ti ka ti ka ti ka ti ka ti ka
Tap: ✗   ✗   ✗   ✗

Sing: tim ka tim ka tim ka tim ka
Tap: ✗   ✗   ✗   ✗

Turn to the Rhythm Jumble Chart on p. 129 and circle the dotted eighth-sixteenth.

Rhythm Jumble Games

On your Theory Worksheets, you have been recording the number of times you used the One-Minute Rhythm Jumble Chart to practice sight reading rhythms. From now on you can play one of the three Rhythm Jumble Games described on p. 130. Play one of these games at least three times before your next lesson. Write your scores in the boxes on your Theory Worksheets. Ask your teacher which one you should start with.

LESSON 14 Theory Worksheet

1 Complete the following charts by filling in the blanks with *one* note.

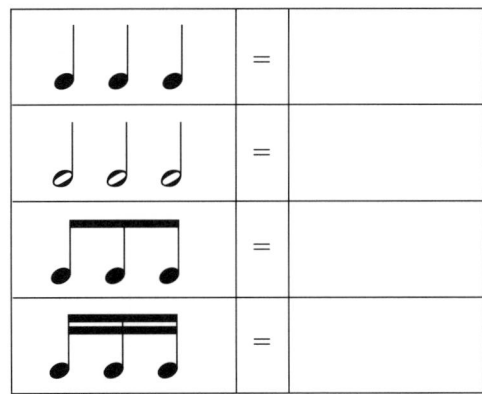

2 For each pair of columns, draw a line from the notes on the left to their corresponding note value on the right.

 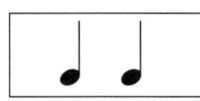  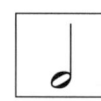

 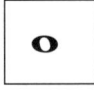 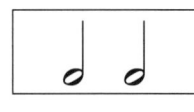   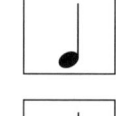

    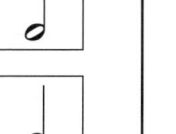  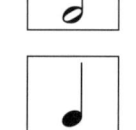

3 Circle the quarter-note beats. Add bar lines according to the time signature.

a)

b)

4 Rewrite the following rhythmic pattern, beaming the eighth notes and sixteenth notes to show the quarter-note beat. Add bar lines.

Rewrite here:

5 Rhythm Jumble Scores ☐ ☐ ☐

72   Lesson 14 Theory Worksheet   Sound Advice Level 4

Ear-Training Worksheet — Lesson 14

1 Interval Identification: You will hear five intervals. The first note of each interval is given. Name the interval and write the second note.

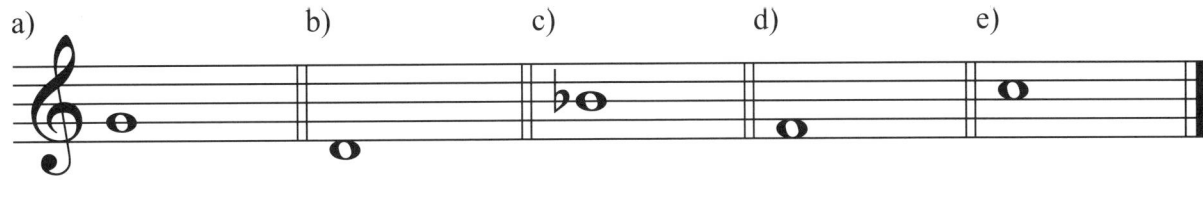

2 Rhythmic Reading:
a) Pause the recording. Sing the following rhythmic pattern while you tap a steady quarter-note beat.
b) Turn to the answer key and sing along with the recording.

3 Rhythmic Dictation: Add the missing notes under the bracket. The pattern will be played twice.

4 Triad Identification: Identify the triads you hear as major or minor.

a)   b)   c)   d)   e)

5 Triads: You will hear a major triad followed by the root, the third, or the fifth of the triad. Write the note that you hear on the staff beside the triad.

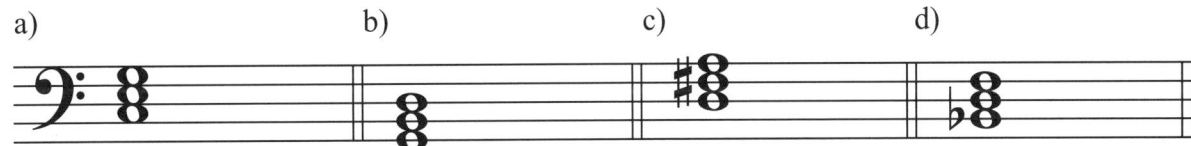

6 Melodic Improvisation: You will hear a two-measure opening.
a) Improvise a two-measure response.
b) Write your response on the staff below. Your melody should end on the tonic.

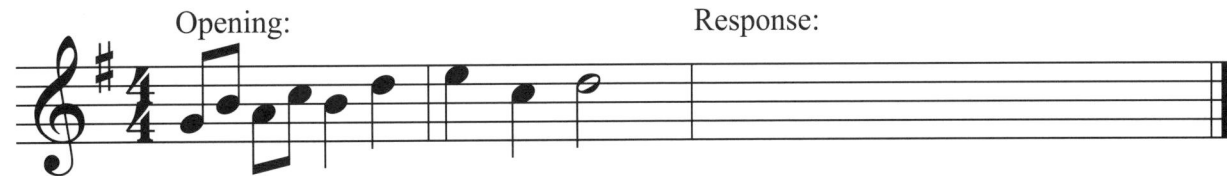

Learning Guide

The Sound of the Descending Major 3rd and Perfect 4th

So far, you have reviewed descending minor 3rds, perfect 5ths, and perfect 8ves. Now you can add two more descending intervals. The descending major 3rd is a new interval in Level 4. The descending perfect 4th is a review from Level 3. You will find song clues for both intervals in the Song Clue Chart on p. 134.

Descending Major 3rd

In major keys, the descending major 3rd is often found at the beginning of a melody between $\hat{3}$ and $\hat{1}$ (mi and do). Sing or play the following melodies.

Westminster Chimes

Swing Low, Sweet Chariot

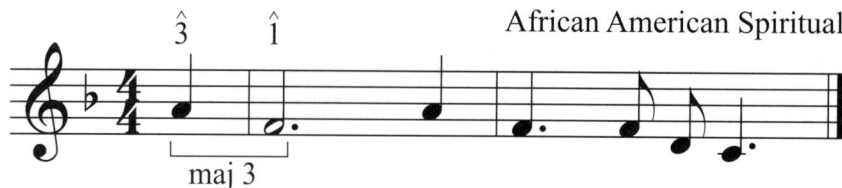

Descending Perfect 4th

The descending perfect 4th is most often heard at the beginning of a melody between $\hat{1}$ and $\hat{5}$ (do and sol). Sing or play the following excerpt.

Eine kleine Nachtmusik

Turn to the Song Clue Chart on p. 134 and put a ✔ beside the descending major 3rd (maj 3) and the descending perfect 4th (P4).

Learning Guide 15

Melodic Inversion

Most composers use some form of imitation in their melodies. When you improvise two-measure responses, you usually imitate the first measure, but you change the last measure so that your response will end on the tonic.

Inversion is a type of imitation. When you invert something you turn it upside down. Melodies can be inverted. Sing or play the following melody.

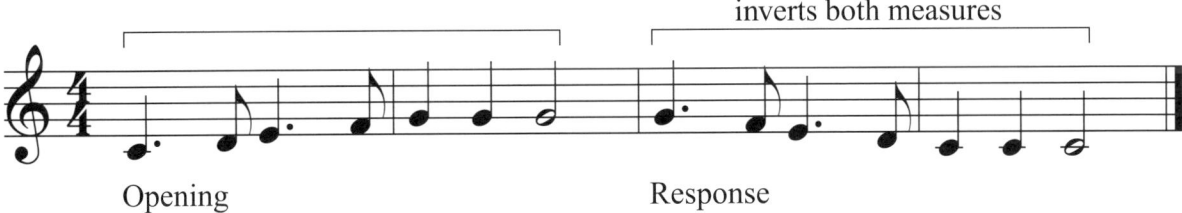

Opening   Response

The opening goes up, and the response goes down. The response, mm. 3–4, is an inversion of mm. 1–2. The melody has been turned upside down. The inverted response is an imitation because the rhythm and the pitches are the same.

Here is another example of melodic inversion. The size of the intervals in the inverted response are the same but the notes move in the opposite direction. The rhythm of the response is the same as the rhythm of the opening.

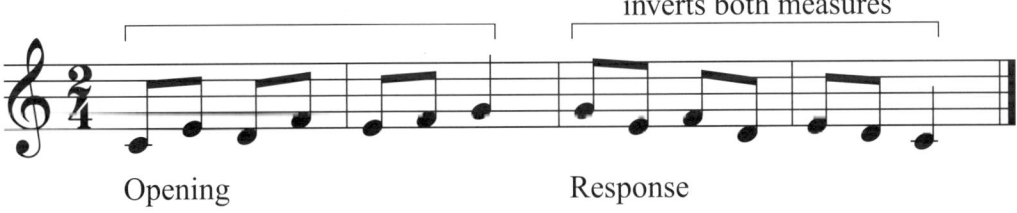

Opening   Response

Not all melodies use inversion, but most melodies have some form of imitation.

From now on, try to vary your melodic responses by using different types of imitation. Choose what you think sounds best based on the given opening.

LESSON 15 Theory Worksheet

1 Write the following key signatures on the grand staff below. Name the relative minor for each key.

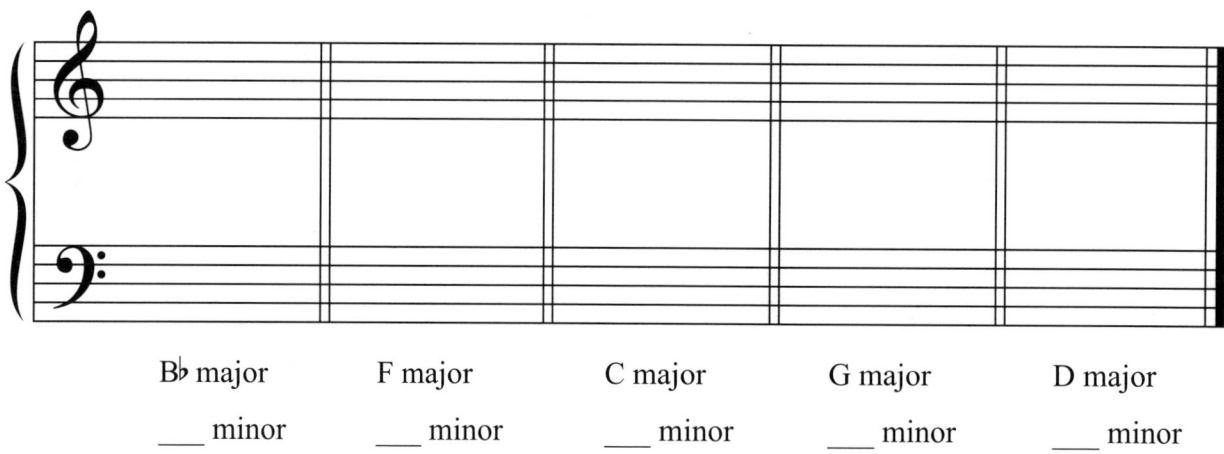

| B♭ major | F major | C major | G major | D major |
| ___ minor | ___ minor | ___ minor | ___ minor | ___ minor |

2 Name the following scale degrees.

a) the dominant of C major _____

b) the tonic of F major _____

c) the leading note of B♭ major _____

d) the dominant of D major _____

3 Study the following excerpt and answer the questions below.

Sonatina, op. 36, no. 2
II
Allegretto
Muzio Clementi
(1752–1832)

Key: _____

a) What does the "II" in the title mean? _____

b) Name the key and number the measures.

c) Add the time signature.

d) Does the melody end on the tonic? _____

e) Mark any examples of imitation with brackets.

Theory Worksheet

LESSON 15

4 Sing or play the following melody. Draw a bracket over any examples of imitation or inversion.

5 Mad Music Scores ☐ ☐ ☐

6 Rhythm Jumble Scores ☐ ☐ ☐

LESSON 15 Ear-Training Worksheet

 1 **Interval Identification:** Identify the intervals you hear as ↗ min 2, maj 2, min 3, maj 3, P4, P5, maj 6, maj 7, P8, ↘ min 3, maj 3, P4, P5, or P8.

a) b) c) d) e)

f) g) h) i) j)

 2 **Sight Singing:**
a) Pause the recording. Sing the following melody while you tap a steady quarter-note beat.
b) Turn to the answer key and sing along with the recording.

 3 **Rhythm Clapback:** Clap the *rhythm* of the melody you hear from memory. Record the number of times you listened.

 4 **Melodic Dictation:** Add the missing notes under the bracket. The melody will be played twice.

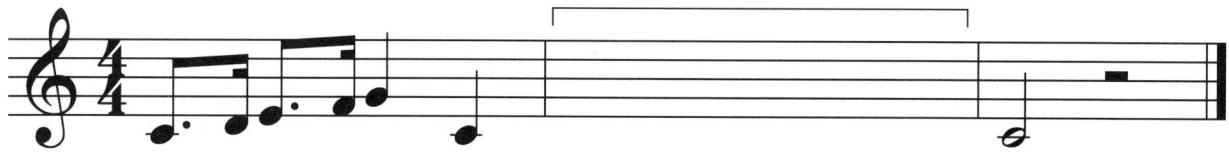

 5 **Melodic Improvisation:** You will hear a two-measure opening.
a) Improvise a two-measure response.
b) Write your response on the staff below. You may wish to use inversion. Your melody should end on the tonic.

Opening: Response:

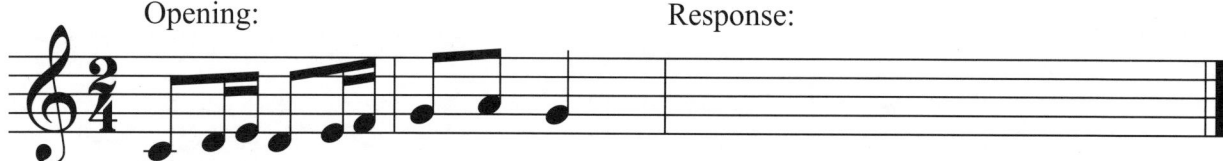

Learning Guide — Lesson 16

Italian Terms

Composers all over the world use Italian terms to tell us how fast, slow, loud, or soft they want their music to be played. If you own (or can borrow) a music dictionary, look up the Italian terms you find in the music you are studying.

Tempo Markings

Music can be fast, slow, or any speed in between. We use the word **tempo** to refer to the speed of music. Here are some common Italian terms for slow to moderate tempos.

Term	Definition
largo	slow and stately
adagio	slow—between *largo* and *andante*
andante	a walking pace—medium speed, faster than *adagio*
moderato	a moderate speed

Chromatic Notes

A **chromatic note** is a note that does not belong to the key in which the music is written. Chromatic notes are written with accidentals. Composers use chromatic notes to make their music sound more interesting.

Here are two versions of a melody by Mozart. In Example 1, the chromatic notes have been removed. Example 2 is Mozart's original melody. Play them both. Which one do you like better?

Example 1

Minuet in C, K 6
(no chromatic notes)

Wolfgang Amadeus Mozart
(1756–1791)

Sound Advice Level 4

Example 2

Minuet in C, K 6
(original)

Wolfgang Amadeus Mozart
(1756–1791)

To learn the sound of chromatic notes, follow these two steps:

1) Sing the first five notes of the C major scale up and down.

2) Sing these notes again, but this time, fill in the whole steps with semitones. The notes you add are chromatic notes.

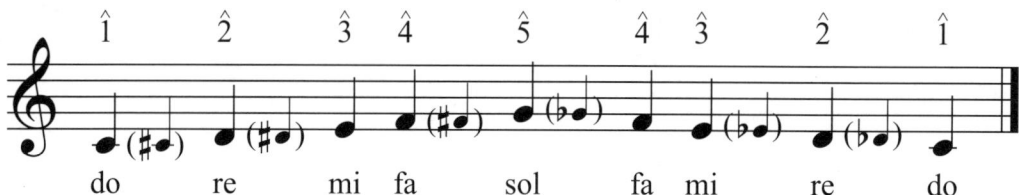

Remember that in a major scale, there is no chromatic note between $\hat{3}$ and $\hat{4}$ (mi and fa) because the distance between these two scale degrees is a half step.

You can sing this exercise using pitch syllables for the chromatic notes. (See the Appendix on pp. 167–168 for information on syllable systems.)

Theory Worksheet

Lesson 16

1 Identify each definition as true or false by writing T or F in the blank box.

Term	Definition	T or F
adagio	a moderate speed	
moderato	fast and lively	
andante	a walking pace	
largo	slow and stately	

2 Write a whole step above each of the following notes.

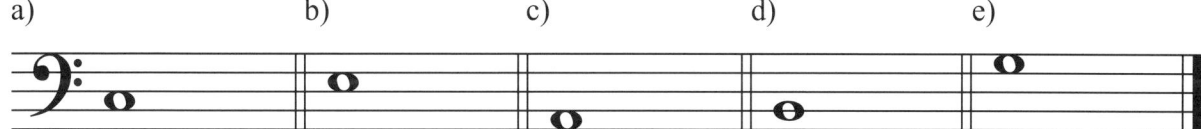

3 Circle the quarter-note beats. Add bar lines according to the time signatures.

4 Circle the quarter-note beats, then add the correct time signature.

5 Circle the chromatic note that appears in one of the melodies on this page.

6 Rhythm Jumble Scores

Sound Advice Level 4   Lesson 16 Theory Worksheet

LESSON 16 — Ear-Training Worksheet

1 **Interval Identification:** Identify the intervals you hear as ↗ min 2, maj 2, min 3, maj 3, P4, P5, maj 6, maj 7, P8, ↘ min 3, maj 3, P4, P5, or P8.

a)　　　　b)　　　　c)　　　　d)　　　　e)

f)　　　　g)　　　　h)　　　　i)　　　　j)

2 **Sight Singing:**
a) Pause the recording. Sing the following melody while you tap a steady quarter-note beat.
b) Turn to the answer key and sing along with the recording.

3 **Editing:** You will hear five pairs of notes. The first note of each pair will be played as written. Based on what you hear, add a sharp, flat, or natural to the *second* note. Each pair of notes will be played twice.

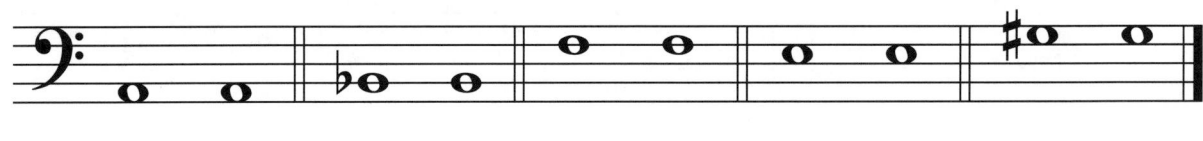

First note:　A　　　B♭　　　F　　　E　　　G♯

4 **Rhythmic Dictation:**
a) Clap the *rhythm* of the melody you hear from memory.
b) Write it in the space below. The rhythm is in 4/4 time.

Ear-Training Worksheet

LESSON 16

 5 **Melodic Dictation:** Add the missing notes under the bracket. The melody will be played twice.

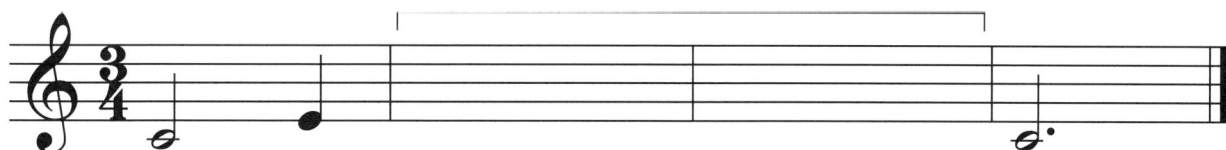

 6 **Melodic Improvisation:** You will hear a two-measure opening.
  a) Improvise a two-measure response.
  b) Write your response on the staff below. Your melody should end on the tonic.

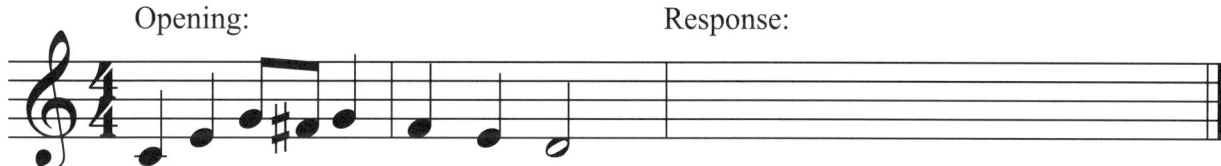

Lesson 17 Learning Guide

More Tempo Markings

Here are some common Italian terms for faster tempos.

Term	Definition
allegretto	fairly fast but slower than *allegro*
allegro	fast and lively
presto	faster than *allegro*

Tonic and Dominant Triads

You have learned that the first note of a scale is called the **tonic** and the fifth note of a scale is called the **dominant**.

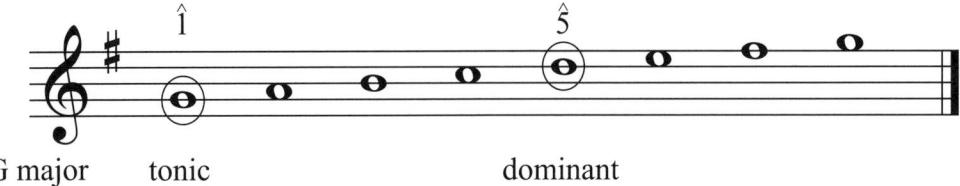

G major   tonic   dominant

Triads can be built on the tonic and dominant notes of a scale. In major keys, the **tonic triad** and the **dominant triad** are both major triads.

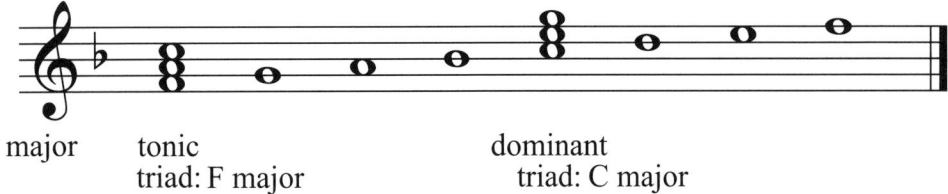

F major   tonic   dominant
           triad: F major   triad: C major

Chords are often labeled with Roman numerals.
- The Roman numeral for 1 is I. The symbol for a tonic triad is I.
- The Roman numeral for 5 is V. The symbol for a dominant triad is V.

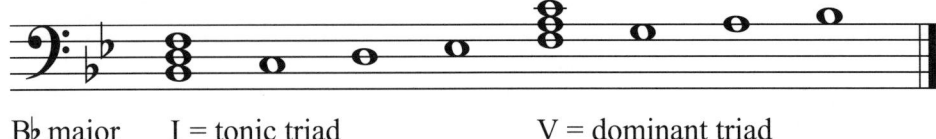

B♭ major   I = tonic triad   V = dominant triad

If you are asked to write tonic or dominant triads using accidentals, follow these three steps:
1) Write the three notes of the triad.
2) Write the sharps or flats of the key signature above the staff.
3) Cross out each sharp or flat as you add the accidental.

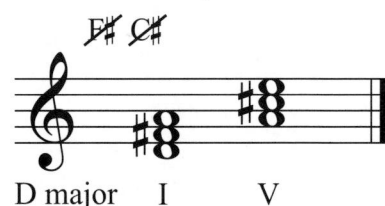

D major   I   V

Theory Worksheet

LESSON 17

1 Fill in the blanks in the following sentences.
   a) The dominant of G major is _____.
   b) The tonic of A minor is _____.
   c) The dominant of D major is _____.
   d) The tonic of E minor is _____.
   e) The dominant of B♭ major is _____.

2 Write the following triads using accidentals instead of a key signature. Label each triad using Roman numerals.
   a) The tonic triad of B♭ major
   b) The dominant triad of G major
   c) The tonic triad of F major
   d) The dominant triad of D major

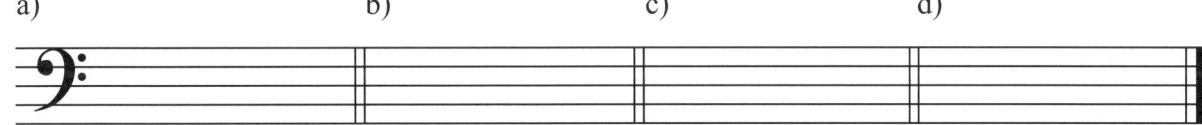

3 Arrange the following Italian terms in order from the slowest to the fastest tempo.
moderato, presto, adagio, allegro, andante, allegretto, largo

   a) _____
   b) _____
   c) _____
   d) _____
   e) _____
   f) _____
   g) _____

4 Name the following intervals. Remember to think in the major scale and key of the lower note.

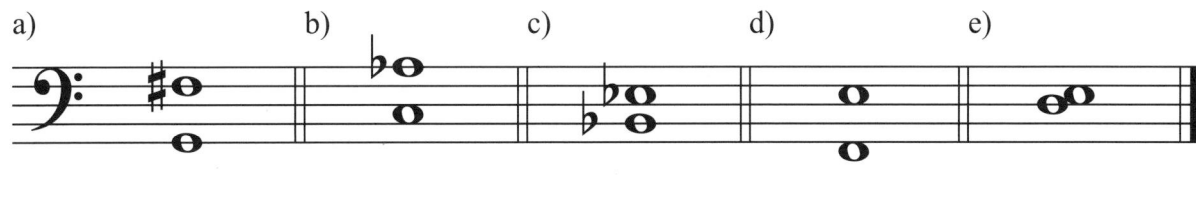

LESSON 17 Theory Worksheet

5 Complete the following chart.

Minor Key	Relative Major	The key signature shared by both keys
B		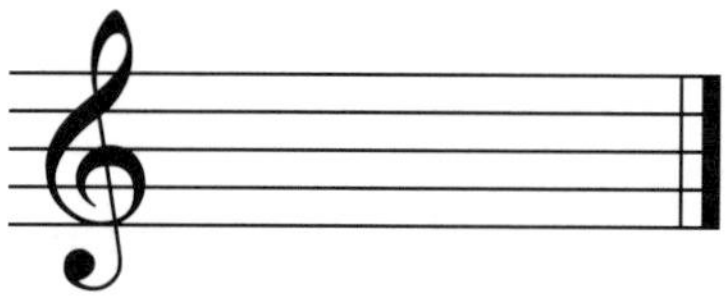
E		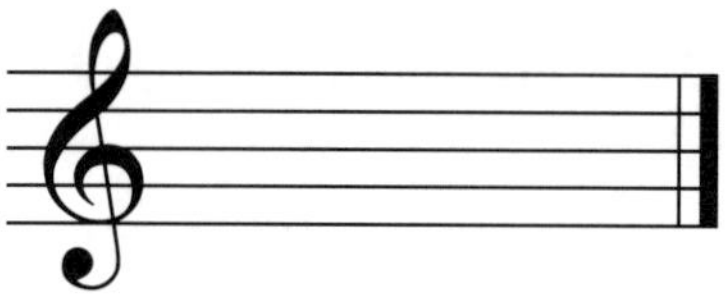
D		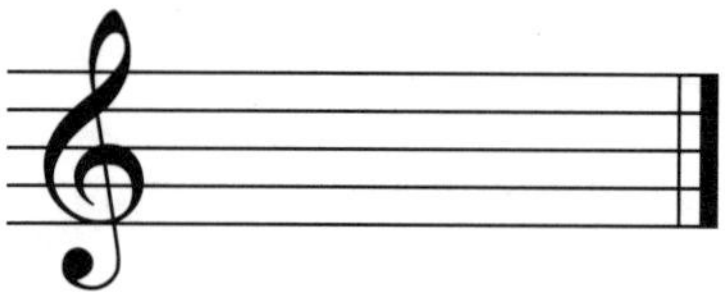
A		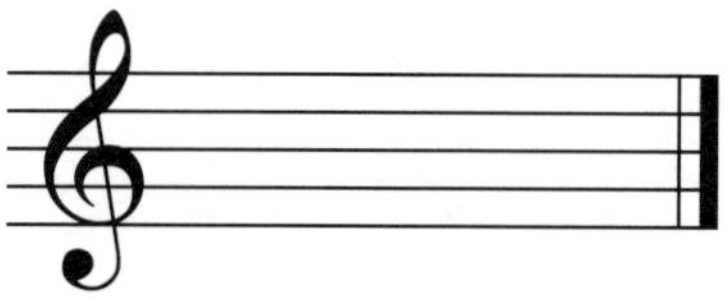
G		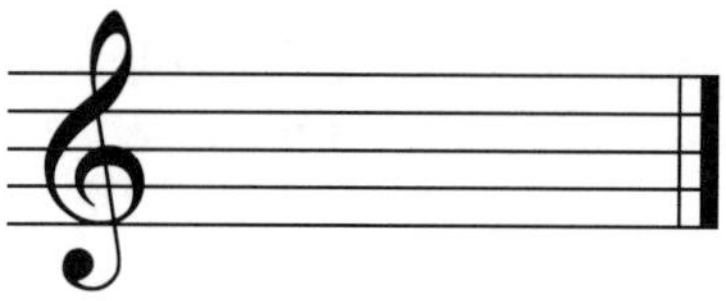

6 Mad Music Scores ☐ ☐ ☐

Ear-Training Worksheet

LESSON 17

 1 **Interval Identification:** Identify the intervals you hear as ↗ min 2, maj 2, min 3, maj 3, P4, P5, maj 6, maj 7, P8, ↘ min 3, maj 3, P4, P5, or P8.

a) b) c) d) e)

f) g) h) i) j)

 2 **Sight Singing:**
a) Pause the recording. Sing the following melody while you tap a steady quarter-note beat.
b) Turn to the answer key and sing along with the recording.

 3 **Rhythmic Dictation:**
a) Clap the *rhythm* of the melody you hear from memory.
b) Write it in the space below. The rhythm is in 2/4 time.

 4 **Melodic Dictation:** Add the missing notes under the bracket. The melody will be played twice.

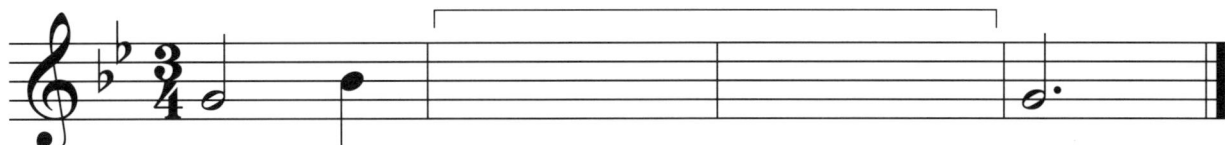

 5 **Melodic Improvisation:** You will hear a two-measure opening.
a) Improvise a two-measure response.
b) Write your response on the staff below. You may wish to use inversion. Your melody should end on the tonic.

Learning Guide

The Sound of Descending Major and Minor 2nds

In this lesson, you will add two more descending intervals to your ear-training exercises. The descending major 2nd is a review from Level 3. The descending minor 2nd is new for Level 4.

Descending Major 2nd

In major keys, the descending major 2nd is often heard at the beginning of a melody between $\hat{3}$ and $\hat{2}$ (mi and re). Two familiar examples are the children's songs "Three Blind Mice" and "Mary Had a Little Lamb."

You may also find a descending major 2nd at the beginning of a melody between $\hat{5}$ and $\hat{4}$ (sol and fa). Here it is in the Christmas carol "Deck the Halls."

Deck the Halls

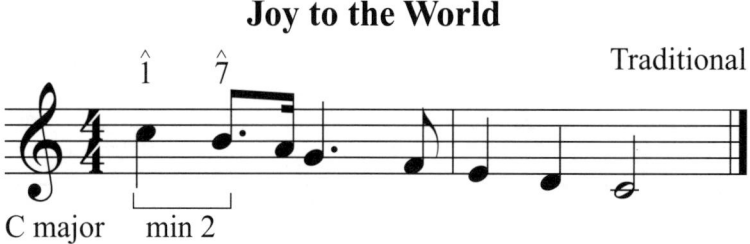

Descending Minor 2nd

A descending minor 2nd is often heard at the beginning of a melody between $\hat{1}$ and $\hat{7}$ (do and ti). Here it is in the Christmas carol "Joy to the World."

Joy to the World

You may also hear a descending minor 2nd in melodies that use a chromatic note below $\hat{5}$, creating a minor 2nd between $\hat{5}$ and $\sharp\hat{4}$ (sol to fi). Here it is at the beginning of Beethoven's well-known piano piece, *Für Elise*.

Für Elise, WoO 59

Turn to the Song Clue Chart on p. 134 and put a ✔ beside the descending major 2nd and the descending minor 2nd.

The Dotted Quarter-Note Beat

All the meters you have learned so far are based on the quarter-note beat. The time signatures all have 4 on the bottom: 2/4, 3/4, 4/4. However, as you have probably noticed in the music you sing or play, the bottom number of a time signature is not always 4.

When the quarter note is the beat, the beat is divisible by two:

However, some meters are based on a dotted quarter-note beat. A dotted quarter note is divisible by three:

Sing the following rhythmic units while you tap a steady dotted quarter-note beat.

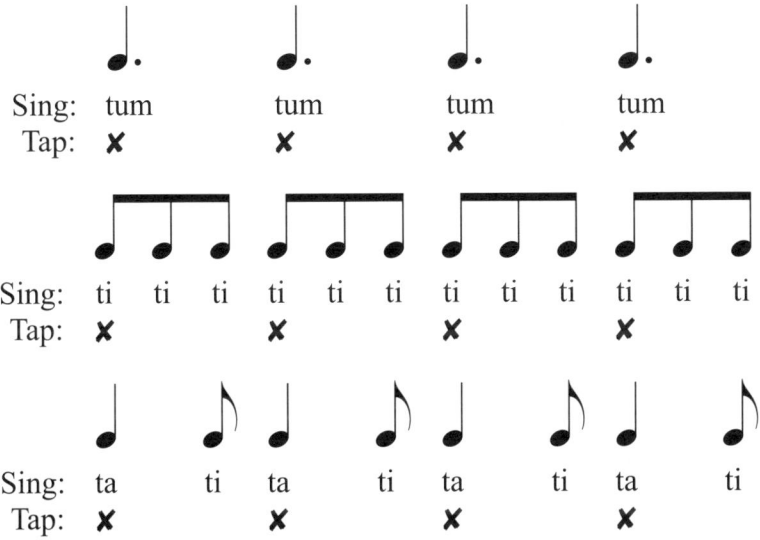

When you circle dotted quarter-note beats, the notes in each circle should be equal to three eighth notes, as shown below.

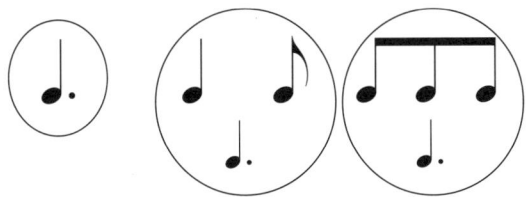

Simple Time and Compound Time

In **simple time** (or simple meter), the beat is divisible by two (for example, the quarter-note beats in 2/4, 3/4, and 4/4).

In **compound time** (or compound meter), the beat is divisible by three (for example, the dotted quarter-note beats you tapped above). In compound time, the beat is always based on a dotted note. You will learn more about compound time in Level 5.

LESSON 18 Theory Worksheet

1 Name the following intervals. Think in the major scale and key of the lowest note.

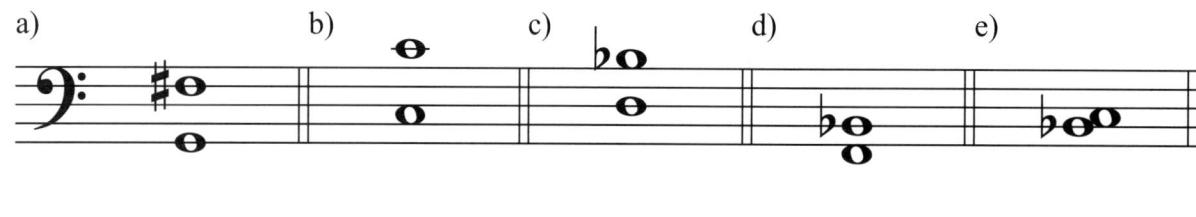

2 For each triad below, name the major key, then identify the triad as tonic (I) or dominant (V). The first one has been done for you.

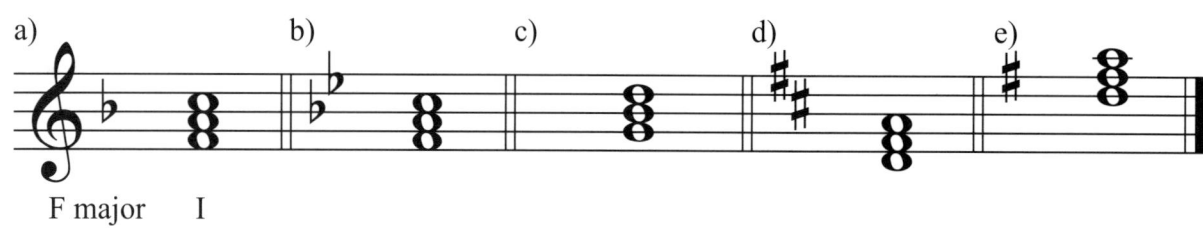

F major   I   ___   ___   ___   ___   ___   ___   ___   ___

3 Circle the quarter-note beats, then add a time signature to each rhythmic pattern.

4 The following rhythmic units are based on either quarter notes or dotted quarter notes. Circle the dotted quarter-note units.

5 Circle the five terms that refer to tempo.

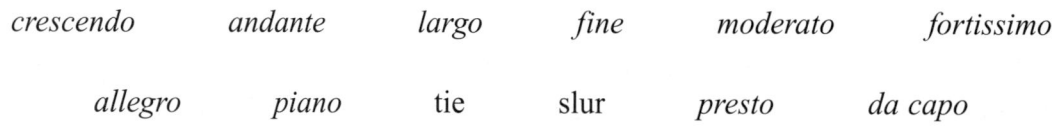

6 Rhythm Jumble Scores ☐ ☐ ☐

Ear-Training Worksheet

LESSON 18

 1 **Interval Identification:** Identify the intervals you hear as ↗ min 2, maj 2, min 3, maj 3, P4, P5, maj 6, maj 7, P8, ↘ min 2, maj 2, min 3, maj 3, P4, P5, or P8.

a)   b)   c)   d)   e)

f)   g)   h)   i)   j)

 2 **Sight Singing:**
a) Pause the recording. Sing the following melody while you tap a steady quarter-note beat.

b) Turn to the answer key and sing along with the recording.

 3 **Rhythmic Reading:**
a) Pause the recording. Sing the following rhythmic pattern while you tap a steady dotted quarter-note beat.

b) Turn to the answer key and sing along with the recording.

 4 **Rhythm Singback/Clapback:** Sing, tap, or clap the rhythmic pattern you hear from memory. It is based on the dotted quarter-note beat.

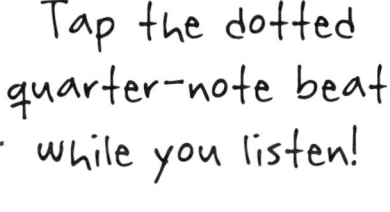

LESSON 18 — Ear-Training Worksheet

 5 **Rhythm Singback/Clapback:** Sing, tap, or clap the rhythmic pattern you hear from memory. It is based on a dotted quarter-note beat.

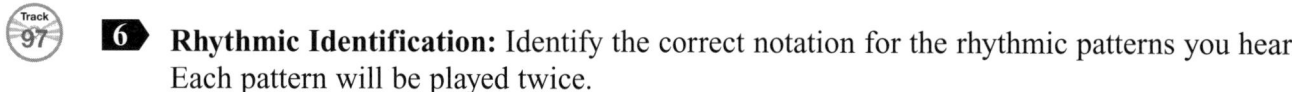 **6** **Rhythmic Identification:** Identify the correct notation for the rhythmic patterns you hear. Each pattern will be played twice.

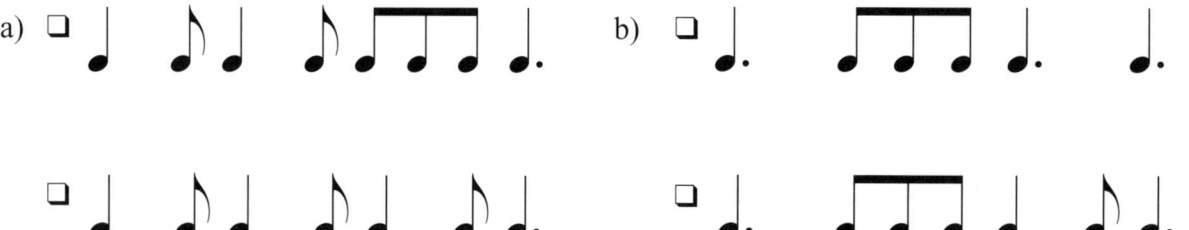

Learning Guide

Lesson 19

A Closer Look at Minor Triads

You have learned to create a minor triad by lowering the middle note (the third) of a major triad by a half step. Study the following major and minor triads.

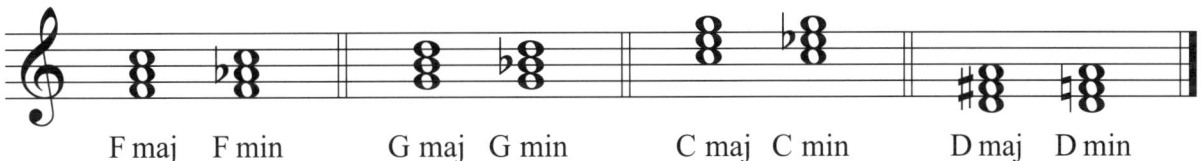

F maj   F min   G maj   G min   C maj   C min   D maj   D min

You can also create a minor triad by using the first, third, and fifth notes of a minor scale ($\hat{1}$–$\hat{3}$–$\hat{5}$).

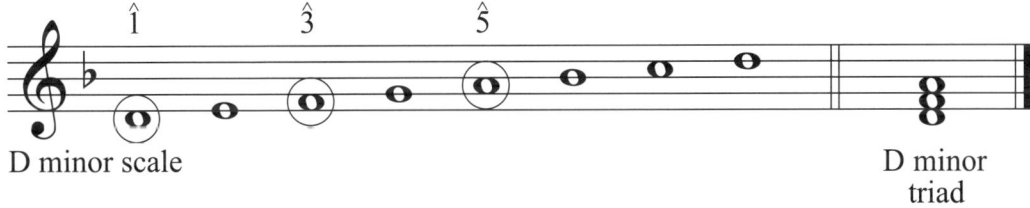

D minor scale   D minor triad

Major triads have a major 3rd on the bottom and a minor 3rd on the top.

Minor triads have a minor 3rd on the bottom and a major 3rd on the top.

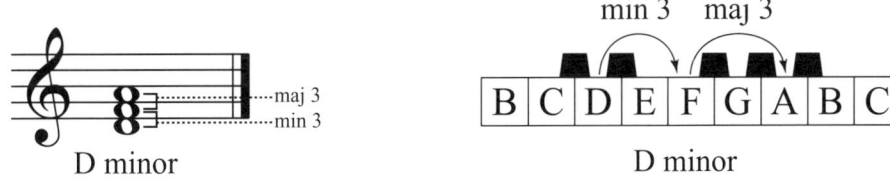

Sound Advice Level 4   Lesson 19 Learning Guide   93

LESSON 19 Learning Guide

Remember that the notes of a triad can be played separately (broken) or together (solid, blocked), and that the bottom note of any triad is called the **root**.

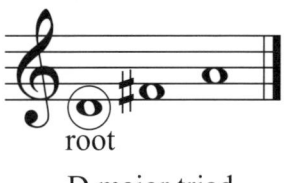

root

D major triad
broken

root

D major triad
solid (blocked)

The Sound of the Descending Minor 6th

The descending minor 6th is a new interval in Level 4.

In major keys, the descending minor 6th is often heard near the end of a melody, between $\hat{5}$ and $\hat{7}$ (sol and ti) as in the following example.

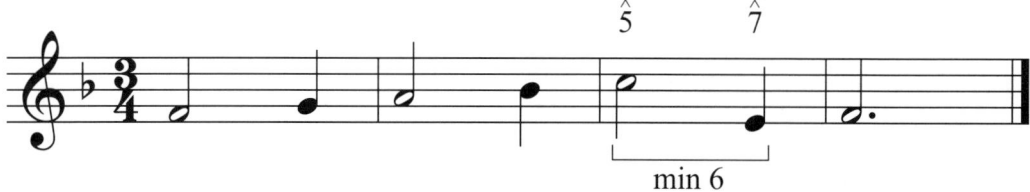

In minor keys, the descending minor 6th is often heard at the beginning of a melody, between $\hat{3}$ and $\hat{5}$ (mi and sol). Examples include the theme from the movie *Love Story* and the song "Please Don't Talk About Me When I'm Gone."

Turn to the Song Clue Chart on p. 134 and put a ✔ beside the descending minor 6th.

Theory Worksheet — Lesson 19

1 Complete the following chart.

Major Key	Relative Minor	The key signature shared by both keys
B♭		
C		
D		
F		
G		

2 Write the following triads in broken form, using key signatures.

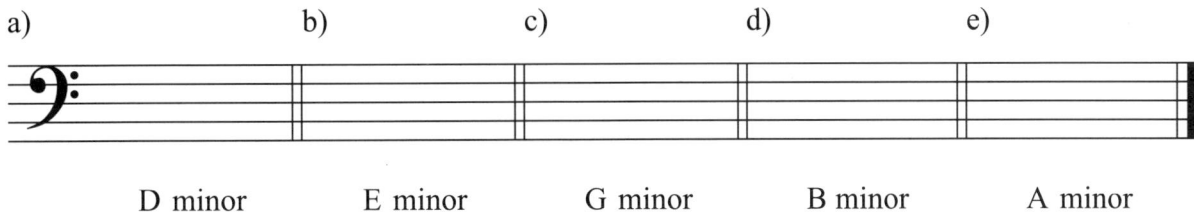

a) D minor   b) E minor   c) G minor   d) B minor   e) A minor

3 Bracket and identify the major and minor 3rds in each of the following triads. The first one has been done for you.

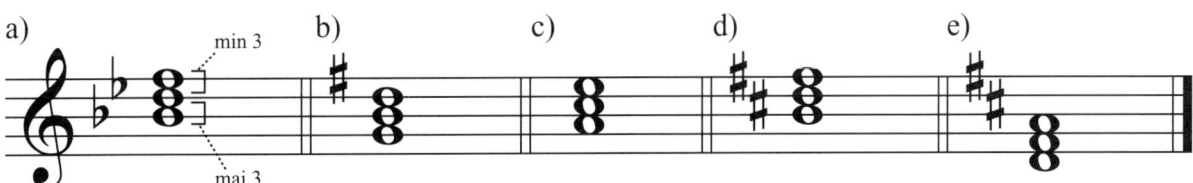

LESSON 19 Theory Worksheet

4 Circle the dotted quarter-note beats in the following rhythmic pattern.

5 Rewrite the following melody, beaming the notes to show the quarter-note beat. Make sure the stems go in the correct direction. Add bar lines.

Polonaise in G minor

Anon.

6 For each pair of columns, draw a line from each group on the left to its corresponding note value on the right.

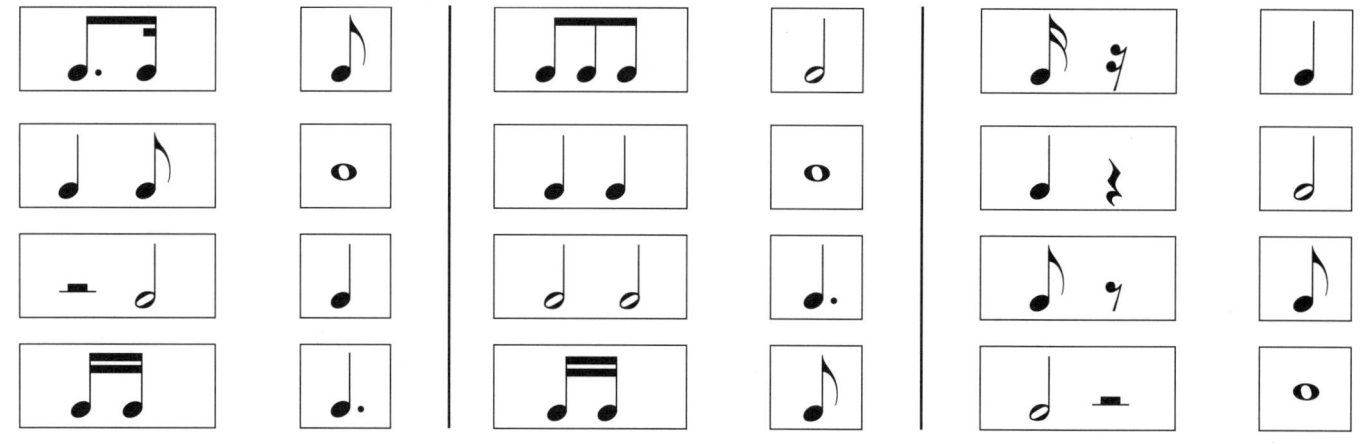

7 Circle the quarter-note beats in the following example, then add bar lines.

8 Mad Music Scores ☐ ☐ ☐

LESSON 19
Ear-Training Worksheet

 1 **Interval Identification:** Identify the intervals you hear as ↗ min 2, maj 2, min 3, maj 3, P4, P5, maj 6, maj 7, P8, ↘ min 2, maj 2, min 3, maj 3, P4, P5, min 6, or P8.

a)   b)   c)   d)   e)

f)   g)   h)   i)   j)

 2 **Melody Singback/Playback:** Sing the melody you hear from memory, then play it on your instrument. The melody is in the key of D minor, in $\frac{3}{4}$ time.

 3 **Rhythmic Reading:**
a) Pause the recording. Sing the following rhythmic pattern while you tap a steady dotted quarter-note beat.

b) Turn to the answer key and sing along with the recording.

 4 **Rhythm Singback/Clapback:** Sing, tap, or clap the rhythmic pattern you hear from memory. It is based on the dotted quarter-note beat.

LESSON 19 Ear-Training Worksheet

 5 **Rhythmic Identification:** Identify the correct notation for the rhythmic pattern you hear. Each pattern will be played twice.

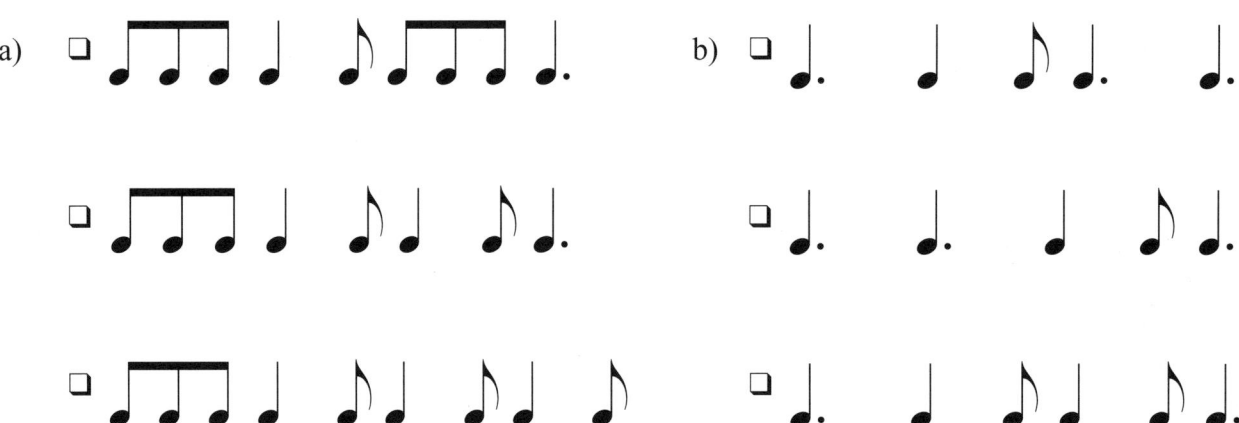

 6 **Editing:**
  a) Add ties where you hear them in the following melody.
  b) Sing the edited melody while you tap a steady quarter-note beat.

Learning Guide

Learning a New Piece: What to Look for First

When you begin to study or perform a piece, always look for three important things at the beginning of the music:
- the **C**lef(s)
- the **K**ey signature
- the **T**ime signature

Remember that these three items appear in alphabetical order (**C**lef, **K**ey, **T**ime) when you write your own melodies.

The Clef
Identifying the clef is simple. So far, you have been reading in the treble clef and the bass clef. These are the two most common clefs.

The Key Signature
It is important to identify the key of the music for two reasons.
1. You need to know which sharps or flats are required.
2. You need to know whether the music is major or minor.

The Time Signature
The time signature determines the meter or accent pattern of the rhythm. So far, you have learned three types of meter: duple (two beats per measure), triple (three beats per measure), and quadruple (four beats per measure).

Identifying the Key of a Melody: Major vs. Minor

To determine whether the key of a melody is major or minor, follow these steps:

1) Read the key signature. Identify the one possible major key and the one possible minor key for that key signature. Write these two choices above the key signature.

2) Sing or play the melody. Does it have a major sound or minor sound? Do you hear scale patterns or triad patterns that belong to one of your choices?

3) Look at the last note of the melody. Does it have a "final" sound? If so, that note will be the tonic of the key.

LESSON 20 Learning Guide

Work through the following examples to see how you can use these steps to identify a key:

Example 1

1) The two possible keys are D major and B natural minor.
2) The melody starts with the first three notes of D major scale, and it has a major sound.
3) The last note of the melody is D.

Key: This melody is in D major.

Example 2

1) The two possible keys are D major and B natural minor.
2) The first measure outlines the B minor triad, and the melody has a minor sound.
3) The last note of the melody is B.

Key: This melody is in B natural minor.

New Rhythmic Unit

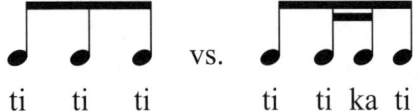

This new unit is based on a dotted quarter-note beat. It is easy to learn when you compare it to the sound of the dotted quarter-note unit made up of three eighth notes:

ti ti ti	ti ti ka ti

Sing the following rhythms while you tap a steady dotted quarter-note beat.

Sing: ti ti ti   ti ti ka ti   ti ti ti   ti ti ka ti
Tap: ✗   ✗   ✗   ✗

Theory Worksheet — Lesson 20

1. Draw a line from each tonic note on the left to its dominant note on the right. The first one has been done for you.

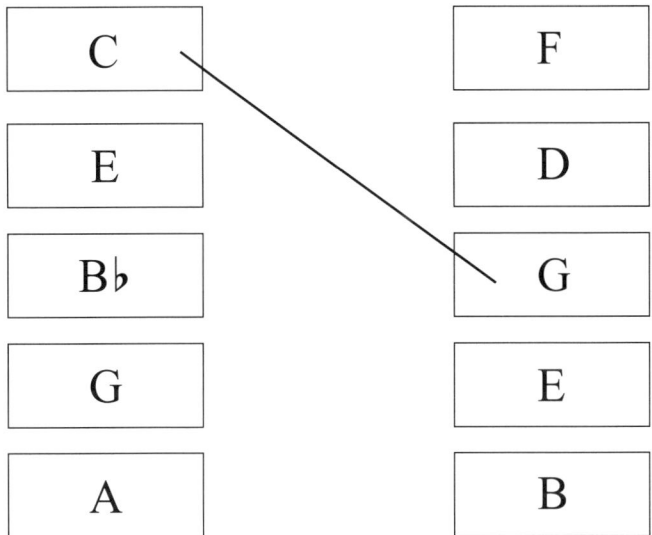

2. Write the letter of the correct definition in the box beside each term.

piano	
andante	
fermata	
presto	
adagio	
allegro	
forte	

A   loud

B   fast and lively

C   slow

D   very fast

E   hold the note longer

F   moderate walking pace

G   soft

3. Draw a line from each time signature to its correct accent pattern.

- 3/4
- C
- 2/4

- ╱ ⌣
- ╱ ⌣ ⌣
- ╱ ⌣ — ⌣

LESSON 20 Theory Worksheet

4 For each column, draw a line from each group on the left to its corresponding note value on the right.

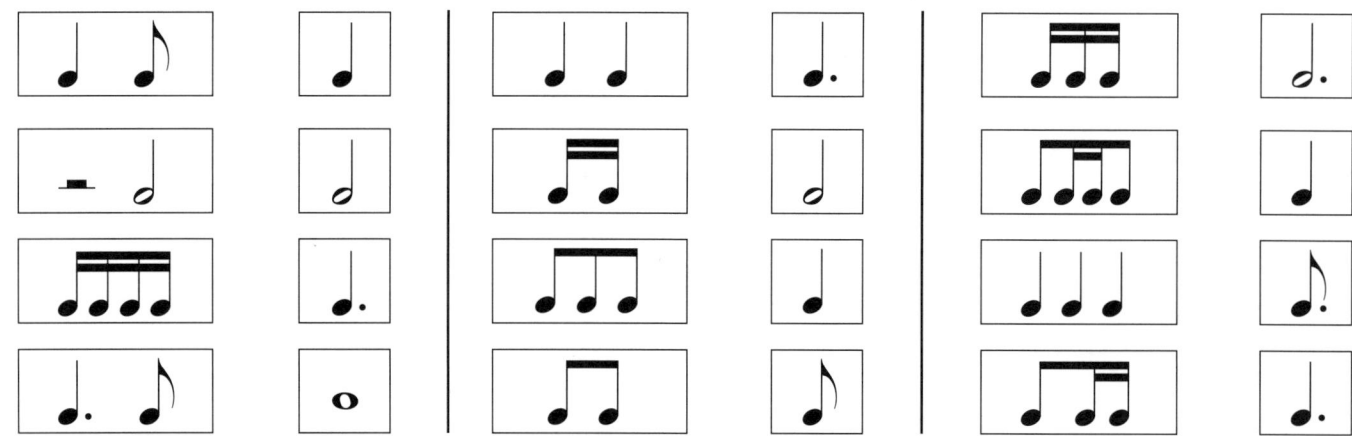

5 Name the key of the following melody by answering these questions:

a) Write the two key choices in the circle above the staff

b) Sing the melody. Does it sound major or minor? _____

c) Circle any scale or triad patterns on the music.

d) Does the last note of this melody sound final? _____

e) What is the name of the last note? _____

f) What is the key of this melody? _____

Key:_____

6 Rhythm Jumble Scores [ ] [ ] [ ]

Ear-Training Worksheet

LESSON 20

1) Interval Identification: Identify the intervals you hear as ↗ min 2, maj 2, min 3, maj 3, P4, P5, maj 6, maj 7, P8, ↘ min 2, maj 2, min 3, maj 3, P4, P5, min 6, or P8.

a)   b)   c)   d)   e)

f)   g)   h)   i)   j)

2) Sight Singing:
a) Pause the recording. Sing the following melody while you tap a steady quarter-note beat.

b) Turn to the answer key and sing along with the recording.

3) Triads: You will hear a minor triad followed by the root, the third, or the fifth of the triad. Write the note that you hear on the staff the each triad.

a)   b)   c)   d)

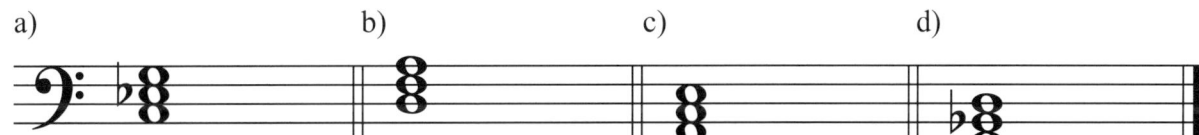

4) Rhythmic Reading:
a) Pause the recording. Sing the following rhythmic pattern while you tap a steady dotted-quarter-note beat.

b) Turn to the answer key and sing along with the recording.

LESSON 20 Ear-Training Worksheet

 5. Error Detection:
   a) Circle any differences you hear in the following melody.

   b) Rewrite the melody to show how it was played on the recording.

 6. Melodic Improvisation: You will hear a two-measure opening.
   a) Improvise a two-measure response.

   b) Write your response on the staff below. Your melody should end on the tonic.

Learning Guide

Musical Texture

The word **texture** is used to describe how music is woven together. You can identify a musical texture by listening, or by looking at the music. Texture is one feature you can use to identify the historical period in which a piece of music may have been written.

Polyphonic Texture

Music that features two or more melodic lines played together has a **polyphonic** texture. The word **counterpoint** is also used to describe this type of music.

In **imitative counterpoint,** the melodic lines in a polyphonic texture imitate one another. Examples of imitative counterpoint include rounds and canons.

The following excerpt by Handel has two independent melodic parts. Therefore, it has a polyphonic texture. It is in imitative counterpoint because the lower part imitates the upper part.

Air in B flat Major, HWV 471

The following excerpt by Bach also has a polyphonic texture. It is not in imitative counterpoint because the two independent parts do not imitate each other.

Minuet in D Minor, BWV Anh. 132

Lesson 21 Learning Guide

Homophonic Texture

Music that features one melodic line with an accompaniment has a **homophonic** texture.

The following excerpt by Diabelli is homophonic; it has a single melody in the upper part and a broken-chord (Alberti bass) accompaniment in the lower part.

Sonatina in F Major

Anton Diabelli
(1781–1858)

Theory Worksheet — Lesson 21

1) Write the following scales in whole notes.
   a) B♭ major, ascending, using accidentals instead of a key signature

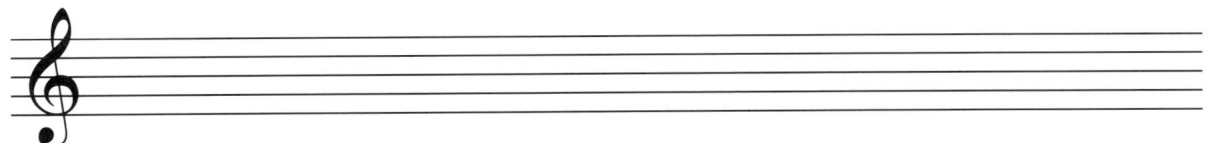

   b) D natural minor, descending, using accidentals instead of a key signature

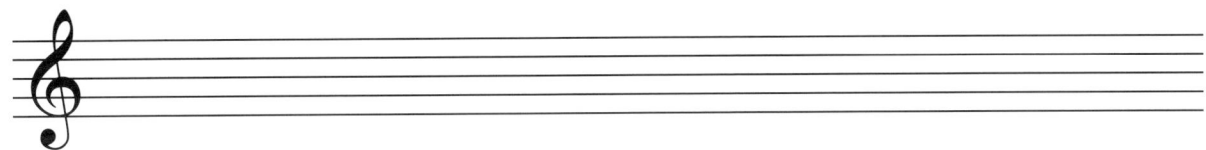

   c) B natural minor, ascending and descending, using a key signature

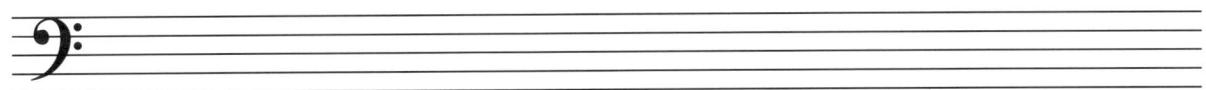

2) Study the following example and answer the questions below.

Rigadoon in A Minor

William Babell
(1690–1723)

Key: _____

   a) Name the key.
   b) Number the measures.
   c) What are the composer's birth and death dates? _____
   d) What type of texture does this music have? _____
   e) In which measure does the lower part begin to imitate the upper part? _____
   f) Is this imitative counterpoint? _____

LESSON 21 Theory Worksheet

2 Study the following excerpt, then answer the questions below.

Waltz

Carl Maria von Weber
(1786–1826)

Key:_____ I_____   I_____   I_____

a) Name the key and number the measures.

b) What does ♩ = 132 – 144 mean?

c) Define the term *allegretto*. _____

d) Is the right-hand part a melody that could exist on its own? _____

e) Is the left-hand part a melody that could exist on its own? _____

f) Is the texture polyphonic or homophonic? _____

g) This example is made up entirely of tonic (I) and dominant (V) chords. In mm. 1, 2, and 4, the chords have been labeled for you. Label the chord in m. 3 on the score. HINT: Look at the notes in *both* clefs.

3 Mad Music Scores ☐ ☐ ☐

Ear-Training Worksheet

LESSON 21

 1 **Interval Identification:** You will hear five intervals. The first note of each interval is given. Name the interval and write the second note.

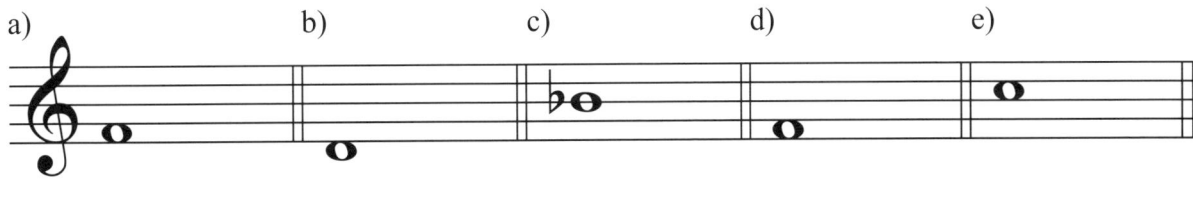

 2 **Melody Singback/Playback:** Sing the melody you hear from memory, then play it on your instrument. The melody is in E minor, in $\frac{3}{4}$ time.

I LISTENED ___ TIMES

 3 **Rhythmic Dictation:**
    a) Clap the *rhythm* of the melody you hear from memory.
    b) Write it in the space below. The rhythm is in $\frac{4}{4}$ time.

 4 **Error Detection:**
    a) Circle any differences you hear in the following melody.
    b) Rewrite the melody to show how it was played on the recording.

Sonatina
Erkki Melartin

 5 **Texture Identification:** Identify the texture of the examples you hear as polyphonic or homophonic.

    a) ❏ polyphonic   b) ❏ polyphonic
        ❏ homophonic   ❏ homophonic

Learning Guide

Review of Baroque and Classical Style

Changes in musical style usually happen gradually, over the course of time. In the past 400 year, there have been four major style periods:

Baroque (1600–1750)
Classical (1750–1825)
Romantic (1825–1900)
Contemporary (1900–present)

So far, you have studied the musical styles of the Baroque and the Classical periods. Here is a summary of some of the main characteristics of these two styles.

	Baroque	**Classical**
Texture	polyphonic texture	homophonic texture
Melody	melodic imitation, counterpoint	symmetrical phrasing
Dynamics	terraced dynamics	*crescendo* and *diminuendo*
Instrumental Forms	dance movements (*minuet, allemande, sarabande, gigue*)	absolute music (sonatas, symphonies, sonatinas)
Orchestra	small orchestra, mainly stringed instruments, no conductor	larger orchestra with four standard instrument groups, conductor in front
Keyboard Instruments	harpsichord, clavichord, and organ	fortepiano (an early piano)
Major Composers	J.S. Bach, G.F. Handel, D. Scarlatti, A. Vivaldi	F.J. Haydn, W.A. Mozart, L. van Beethoven

Musical Style of the Romantic Period

Music of the Romantic period was written between 1825 and 1900—about 100–180 years ago. Here are four important features of music from the Romantic period.

Homophonic Texture
Like the music of the Classical period, Romantic music features mainly homophonic textures. However, the texture of Romantic music is usually thicker than that of Classical music, because Romantic composers generally use more instruments, more voices, and more layers of sound.

Increased Expressiveness
Romantic composers were quite specific about how they wanted their music to be performed. They used many more markings than Baroque and Classical composers. Descriptive markings such as *con fuoco* (with fire), *dolente* (weeping), and *maestoso* (majestic); dynamic markings, such as *crescendo* and *diminuendo*; and extreme dynamic ranges, such as ***ppp*** or ***fff*** can often be found in Romantic scores.

Learning Guide 22

Descriptive Titles
Classical composers often used titles such as "sonata" or "symphony" for their instrumental works. Romantic composers also wrote sonatas and symphonies, often with a descriptive title, like *Symphonie fantastique*, to reinforce their musical descriptions of a specific mood, story, or image. Romantic piano pieces also have descriptive titles such as "Fluttering Leaves," "The Wild Horseman," and "Little Bird."

Program Music
Some Romantic composers identified stories or specific pictures and scenes that were depicted in their instrumental works. A piece of instrumental music that includes a written story or scene is called **program music**. Two famous examples are *The Moldau* by Bedřich Smetana and *Symphonie fantastique* by Hector Berlioz.

LESSON 22 Theory Worksheet

1 Write a whole tone above each note.

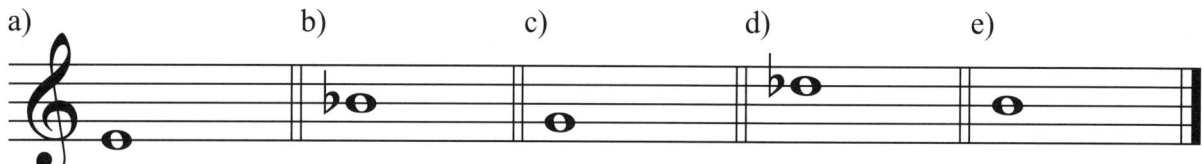

2 Name the following intervals. Think in the major scale and key of the lowest note.

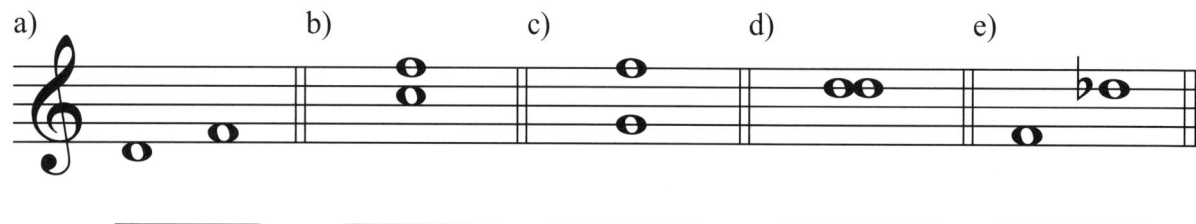

3 Write the following solid triads in whole notes on the staff below. Use a key signature.

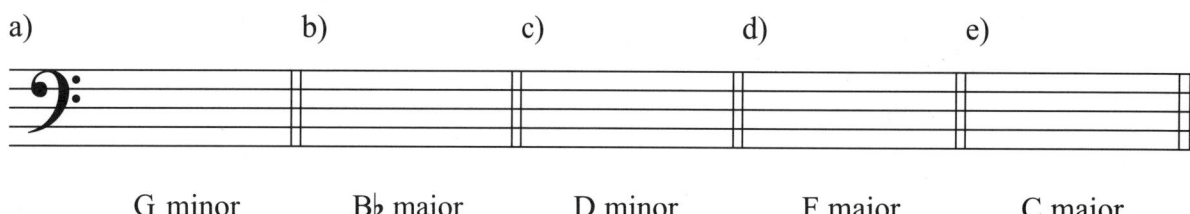

G minor   B♭ major   D minor   F major   C major

4 Circle the quarter-note beats. Add bar lines according to the time signatures.

5 Rhythm Jumble Scores ☐ ☐ ☐

Ear-Training Worksheet

LESSON 22

 1 **Interval Identification:** You will hear five intervals. The first note of each interval is given. Name the interval and write the second note.

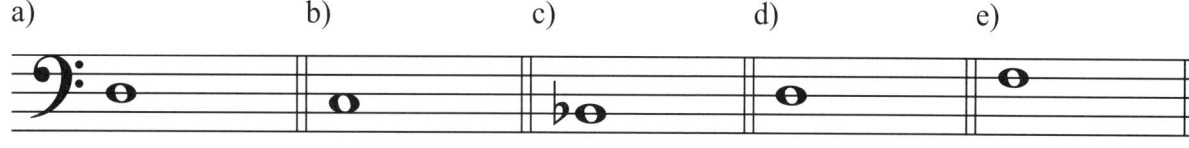

 2 **Melodic Improvisation:** You will hear a two-measure opening.
  a) Improvise a two-measure response.
  b) Write your response on the staff below. Your melody should end on the tonic.

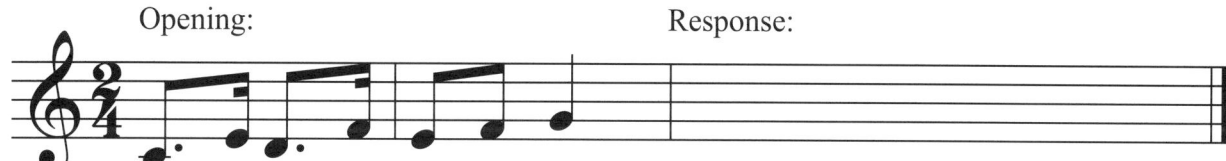

 3 **Rhythmic Dictation:**
  a) Clap the *rhythm* of the melody you hear from memory.
  b) Write it in the space below. The rhythm is in 4/4 time.

 4 **Error Detection:**
  a) Circle any differences you hear in the following melody.
  b) Rewrite the melody to show how it was played on the recording.

Sonatina in F Major

Anton Diabelli
(1781–1858)

 5 **Texture Identification:** Identify the texture of the examples you hear as polyphonic or homophonic.

  a) ❏ polyphonic   b) ❏ polyphonic
     ❏ homophonic   ❏ homophonic

Learning Guide

A Closer Look at Romantic Musical Style: Art Song and Nationalism

Art Song
An **art song** is a work for solo voice and piano. Some composers wrote sets of art songs called **song cycles**. The songs within a song cycle are usually connected by a theme such as love, a journey, or something in nature. German art songs were particularly popular in the Romantic period. A German song is called a *Lied* (plural *Lieder*).

In most Romantic art songs, there is a strong connection between the poetry and the music. Often the piano accompaniment, rather than serving as background music, depicts an aspect of the poetry, such as a galloping horse, a stream, or the wind.

Nationalism
In music, the word **nationalism** refers to the use of folk songs, stories, and dances of the composer's native country. Many Romantic composers used musical elements from their homeland. European national styles found in Romantic repertoire include Hungarian, Polish, Russian, Bohemian, and Scandinavian.

The Piano in the Romantic Period

The 19th-Century Piano
Many improvements were made to the piano during the Romantic period. Frames were made of cast iron, rather than wood, the action of the keys was faster and more responsive to the touch, the strings were thicker and longer, and the keyboard was extended to six and a half octaves. As a result, 19th-century pianos had a rich singing tone and a wide dynamic range. They also stayed in tune longer than the early fortepianos.

Because pianos were made in factories, they were more affordable to middle-class families. There were a number of different models they could choose from, and many families had a piano in the parlor. Printed sheet music was readily available, and piano lessons were in great demand.

The Short Piano Piece
Romantic composers took advantage of the improvements in the piano. In their music they explored the piano's new technical features and expressive possibilities. The most popular type of piano composition was the short piano piece

This type of composition could be a slow, lyrical work or a fast, brilliant showpiece. Typical titles for Romantic piano pieces include prelude, nocturne, intermezzo, and impromptu. Some composers wrote dances, such as Polish *mazurkas* and *polonaises* or Viennese waltzes. Many short piano pieces have descriptive titles (for example, *The Little Bell, From Foreign Lands and People,* or *Spinning Song).*

Theory Worksheet — Lesson 23

1) Play or sing the following two-measure melodic opening, then improvise your own response. Your response should imitate the first measure and end on the tonic.

2) Study the following example and answer the questions below.

Romance

Felix Mendelssohn
(1809–1847)

Andante

a) Name the key. _____

b) Number the measures.

c) Name the composer of this piece. _____

d) What are the composer's dates? _____

e) Name the triad in the bass staff on the first beat of m. 2. _____

f) Identify the texture of this music. _____

g) In which period do you think this might have been written? _____

h) Define the term *andante*. _____

LESSON 23 Ear-Training Worksheet

1. Interval Identification: Identify the intervals you hear as ↗ min 2, maj 2, min 3, maj 3, P4, P5, maj 6, maj 7, P8, ↘ min 2, maj 2, min 3, maj 3, P4, P5, min 6, or P8. Each interval will be played once.

a)   b)   c)   d)   e)

f)   g)   h)   i)   j)

2. Melody Singback/Playback: Sing the melody you hear from memory, then play it on your instrument. The melody is in D minor, in 3/4 time.

3. Melodic Dictation:
a) Sing the melody you hear from memory.
b) Write it on the staff below. The melody is in F major, in 3/4 in time.

I LISTENED ☐ TIMES

4. Triads: You will hear a major triad followed by the root, the third, or the fifth of the triad. Write the note you hear on the staff beside the triad.

a)   b)   c)   d)

5. Texture Identification: Identify the texture of the examples you hear as polyphonic or homophonic.

a) ☐ polyphonic
   ☐ homophonic

b) ☐ polyphonic
   ☐ homophonic

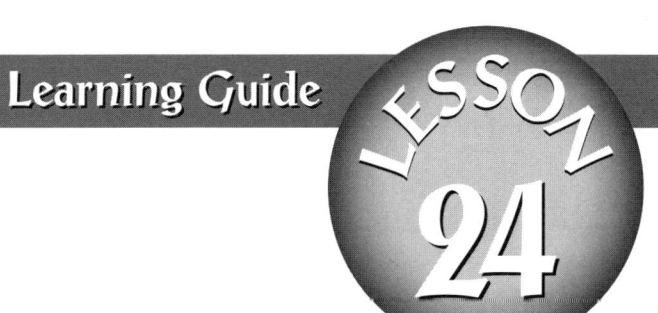

The Romantic Orchestra

A Baroque orchestra in the early 1700's would have had approximately twenty musicians. In Mozart's time, that number might have been as high as forty. During the Romantic period, the largest orchestras had more than a hundred musicians. These larger orchestras were made up of the four instrumental families established during the Classical period: strings, woodwinds, brass, and percussion.

Improvements to many instruments affected the size and sound of the Romantic orchestra. For example, brass instruments now had valves, which extended their chromatic range and made them easier to play. New instruments, including the tuba and the saxophone, were added. The percussion section became larger and more interesting with the addition of new instruments, such as xylophones, gongs, bells, chimes, and castanets. To provide balance, the string section was also enlarged.

With all these resources at their fingertips, Romantic composers experimented with tone color. They used instruments in their highest and lowest registers, creating orchestral effects that would have been unthinkable during the Baroque and Classical periods.

Recommended Listening

The best way to become acquainted with the sound of the Romantic orchestra is to listen to some recordings or attend a concert. Here are a few suggestions of pieces to look for in your local library or on the Internet:

The Nutcracker by Pyotr Il'yich Tchaikovsky
Flight of the Bumble Bee by Nicolai Rimsky-Korsakov
The Moldau by Bedřich Smetena
Symphonie fantastique by Hector Berlioz
Peer Gynt Suite by Edvard Grieg

Composers of the Romantic Period

Franz Schubert (1797–1828)
The music of Franz Schubert bridges the Classical and Romantic periods. As a composer of *Lieder* (German art songs), Schubert made a major contribution to Romantic music. He wrote more than 600 songs, a number of them in cycles. Schubert's piano music includes fifteen sonatas and numerous short piano pieces with titles such as *fantasy, impromptu,* or *moment musical.*

Frédéric Chopin (1810–1849)
Frédéric Chopin was born in Poland but spent his musical career in Paris. His composing activities centered around the piano and he has been called the "poet of the piano" because of his beautiful melodies. Chopin's short piano pieces include etudes (studies), nocturnes, impromptus, preludes, and waltzes. Chopin's nationalism is reflected in his mazurkas and polonaises, both of which are based on Polish dances.

Robert Schumann (1810–1856)
Like Schubert, Robert Schumann was a prolific composer of *Lieder*. He wrote more than 300 songs. He also composed four symphonies and hundreds of short piano pieces, many of them grouped in sets. His wife, Clara Schumann, a famous concert pianist who performed all over Europe, was also a talented composer.

LESSON 24 Theory Worksheet

1 Study the following excerpt and answer the questions below.

The Wild Horseman

Robert Schumann
(1810–1856)

Key:_____

a) Number the measures.

b) Does this melody begin with an upbeat? _____ How many measures are there? _____

c) What are the composer's birth and death dates? _____

d) This piece is based on the dotted quarter-note beat. Circle the beats in the first three measures.

e) Define the dynamic marking *mf*. _____

f) This excerpt is made up of two phrases. Mark the phrases with slurs.

g) Compare the second phrase with the first phrase. Circle the notes in the second phrase that *do not* imitate the first phrase. Include both the treble and bass staves.

h) This piece is in the key of A minor. Name the triad created by the notes in m. 1. _____

i) Is the texture of this music homophonic or polyphonic? _____

j) In which period was this piece written? _____

Ear-Training Worksheet

LESSON 24

 1 **Interval Identification:** Identify the intervals you hear as ↗ min 2, maj 2, min 3, maj 3, P4, P5, maj 6, maj 7, P8, ↘ min 2, maj 2, min 3, maj 3, P4, P5, min 6, or P8. Each interval will be played once.

a)   b)   c)   d)   e)

f)   g)   h)   i)   j)

 2 **Triads:** You will hear a minor triad followed by the root, the third, or the fifth of the triad. Write the note that you hear on the staff beside the triad.

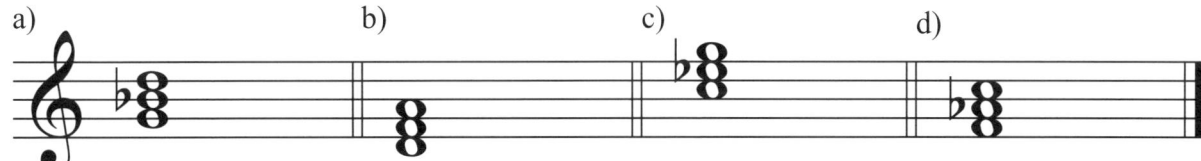

 3 **Melody Singback/Playback:** Sing back the melody you hear from memory, then play it on your instrument. The melody is in the key of B minor, in 3/4 time.

 4 **Melodic Dictation:**
a) Sing the melody you hear from memory.
b) Write it on the staff below. The melody is in D major, in 3/4 time.

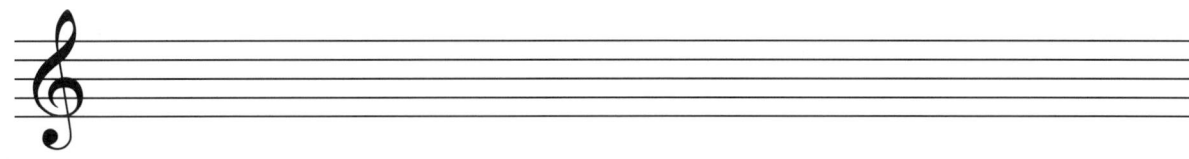

 5 **Error Detection:**
a) Circle any differences you hear in the following melody.
b) Rewrite the melody to show how it was played on the recording.

Theory Examination

Duration: One Hour

Name: _____

10 **1** Name the following notes.

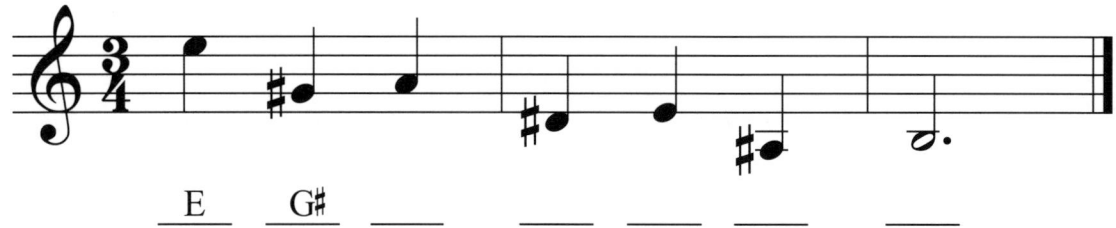

10 **2** Circle the quarter-note beats. Add bar lines according to the time signature.

Theory Examination

10 **3** Write the following scales in whole notes.

a) D major, descending, using a key signature

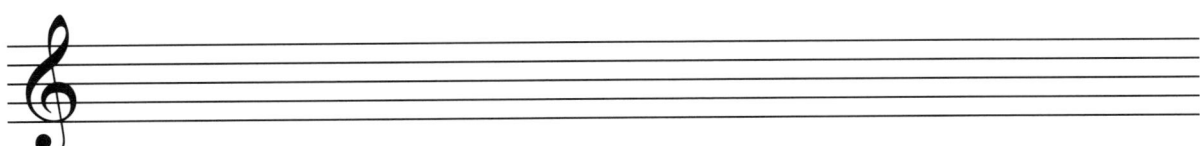

b) G natural minor, ascending, using accidentals instead of a key signature

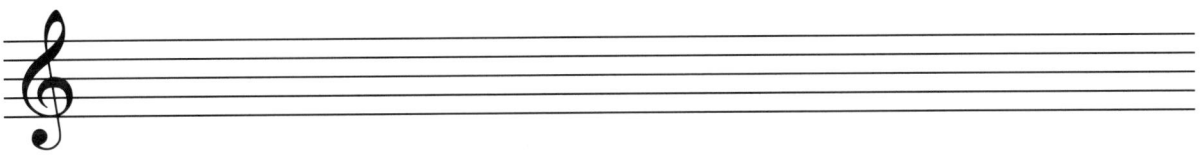

c) B♭ major, descending, using accidentals instead of a key signature

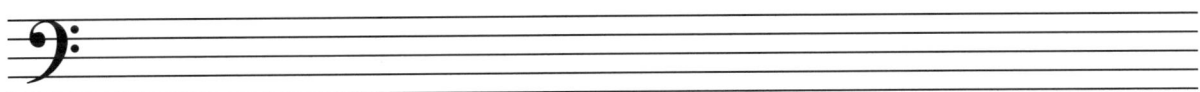

d) E natural minor, ascending, using a key signature

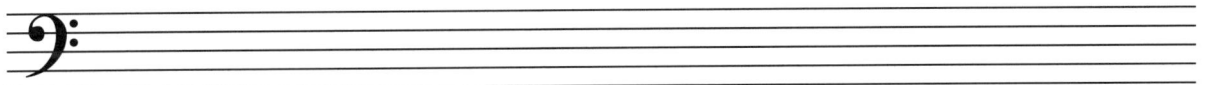

10 **4** Name the following intervals.

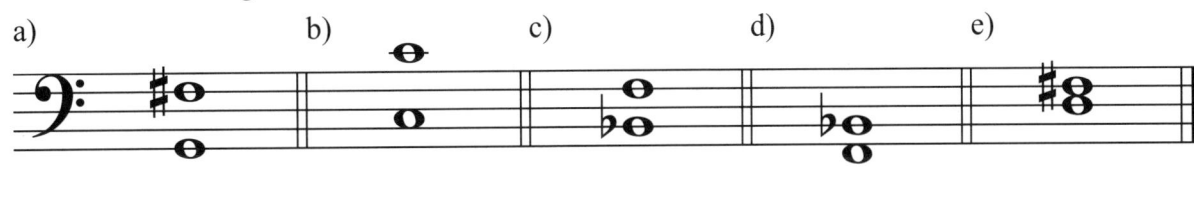

Theory Examination

5 **5** Name the key of each of the following melodies.

a)

Key: _____

b)

Key: _____

c)

Key: _____

d)

Key: _____

5 **6** a) Play or sing the following melodic opening, then improvise a two-measure response

b) Write your response on the staff below. Your response should end on the tonic.

6 **7** Name the key of the following melody. Circle and label the tonic (T), dominant (D), and leading note (LN) each time they occur.

Key: _____

Theory Examination

15 **8** Study the excerpt below, then answer the following questions.

Run and Play

Stephen Brown
(b. 1948)

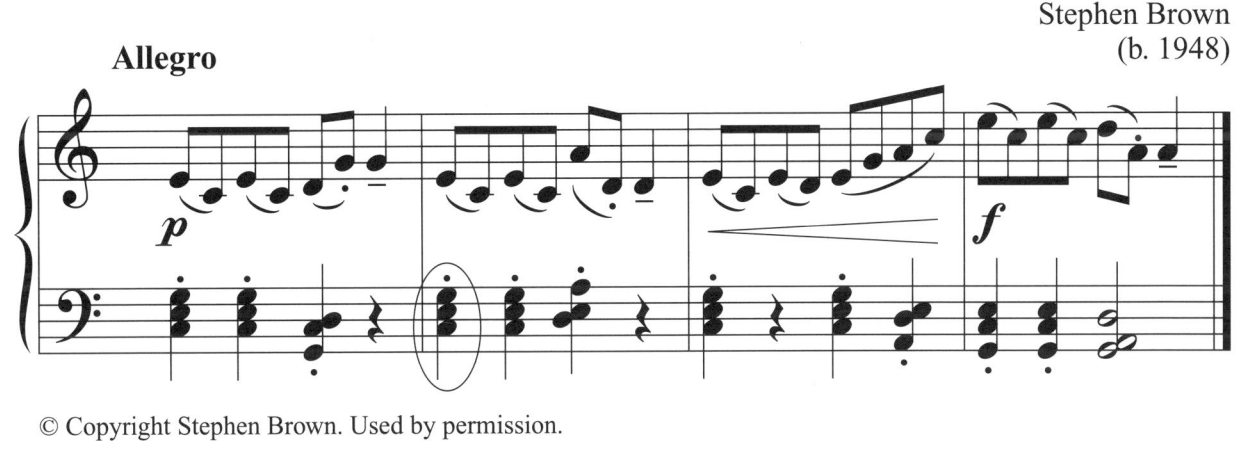

© Copyright Stephen Brown. Used by permission.

a) Add the time signature.

b) Who is the composer of this music? _____

c) How many slurs are in the melody? _____

d) Number the measures.

e) How many measures are there? _____

f) What is the letter name of the highest note in the melody? _____

g) What is the letter name of the lowest note in the melody? _____

h) In which measure is the music the loudest? _____

i) Is the texture of this music polyphonic or homophonic? _____

j) What is the name of the dot on the circled chord in m. 2? _____

k) The title of this piece is *Run and Play*. What makes the music sound playful?

_____

l) Define the following terms and symbols used in this piece:

allegro _____

p _____

f _____

< _____

Theory Examination

5 **9** Rewrite the following rhythmic pattern, beaming the notes to show the quarter-note beat. Add bar lines.

Rewrite here:

5 **10** Circle the five words that refer to tempo.

crescendo *andante* *largo* *fine* *moderato* *fortissimo*

allegro *piano* tie slur *presto* *da capo*

10 **11** For each of the following triads, name the major key and identify the triad as tonic (I) or dominant (V).

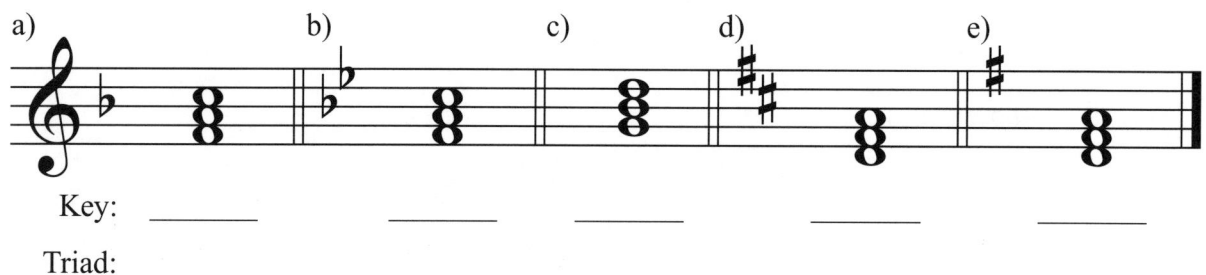

Key: _____ _____ _____ _____ _____

Triad: _____ _____ _____ _____ _____

10 **12** Circle the quarter-note beats in the following melodies, then add time signatures.

100

Melody Master

These are the final Ear-Training Worksheets for Level 4. Spend as much time as necessary to perfect these assignments, then move on to *Sound Advice* Level 5.

Melody Master consists of five sets of melodies. You need to complete all five sets using the three different methods described below. Finish all five sets with Method 1 before you go on to Method 2. Finish the five sets with Method 2 before you move on to Method 3. When you successfully complete of each set, check the box at the bottom of this page to track your progress.

Always record your progress before going on to the next method!

Method 1: Melody Playback—Play What You Hear

Singers and instrumentalists can perform in their range. Each melody will be played twice on the recordings. The tonic triad and the beat are given before each performance. The melodies start on the root, the third, or the fifth of the triad.

Method 2: Sight Singing—Hear What You See

Turn to the Melody Master Answer Key and sight sing all five sets.

Method 3: Melodic Dictation—Write What You Hear

Write each melody on the staff. Each melody will be played twice. The tonic triad and the beat are given before each performance. The melodies start on the root, the third, or the fifth of the triad.

Method 1: Playbacks	Method 2: Sight Singing	Method 3: Melodic Dictation
Set One ❑	Set One ❑	Set One ❑
Set Two ❑	Set Two ❑	Set Two ❑
Set Three ❑	Set Three ❑	Set Three ❑
Set Four ❑	Set Four ❑	Set Four ❑
Set Five ❑	Set Five ❑	Set Five ❑

Melody Master

Set One

a) The following melody is in C major, in 4/4 time.

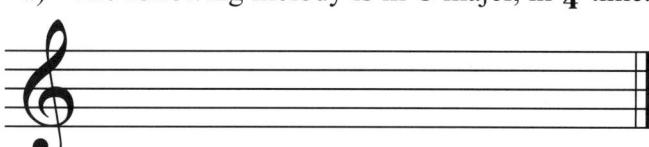

b) The following melody is in F major, in 3/4 time.

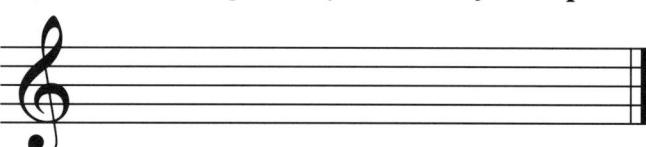

c) The following melody is in G major, in 2/4 time.

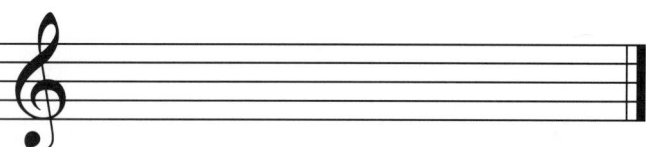

d) The following melody is in D major, in 4/4 time.

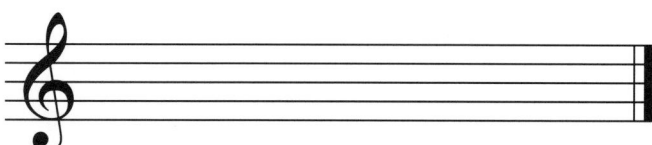

e) The following melody is in B♭ major, in 3/4 time.

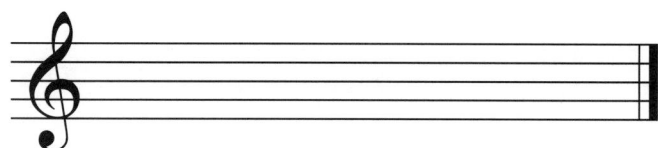

Check the appropriate box on p. 125.

Set Two

a) The following melody is in C major, in 3/4 time.

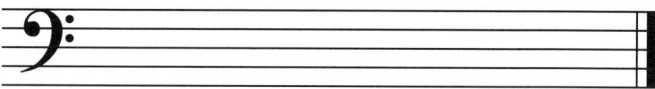

b) The following melody is in D major, in 3/4 time.

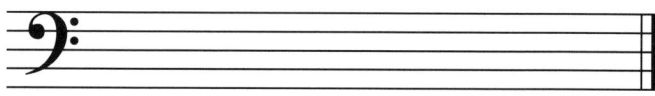

c) The following melody is in F major, in 4/4 time.

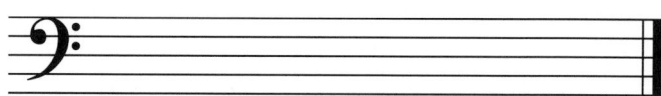

d) The following melody is in G major, in 3/4 time.

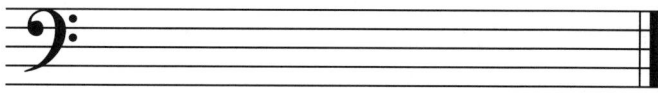

e) The following melody is in B♭ major, in 4/4 time.

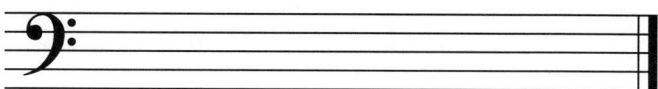

Check the appropriate box on p. 125.

Melody Master

Set Three

a) The following melody is in A minor, in 3/4 time.

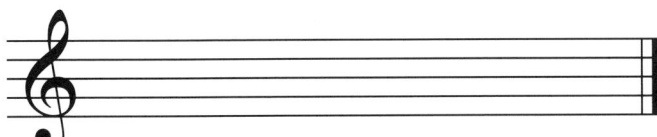

b) The following melody is in D minor, in 4/4 time.

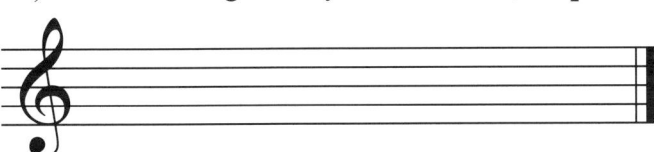

c) The following melody is in E minor, in 4/4 time.

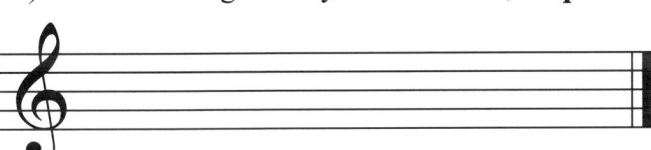

d) The following melody is in G minor, in 3/4 time.

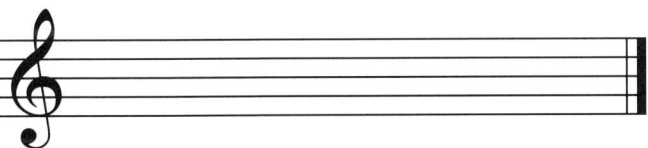

e) The following melody is in A minor, in 4/4 time.

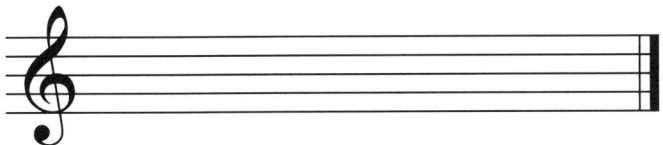

Check the appropriate box on p. 125.

Set Four

a) The following melody is in A minor, in 2/4 time.

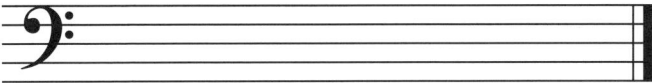

b) The following melody is in G minor, in 2/4 time.

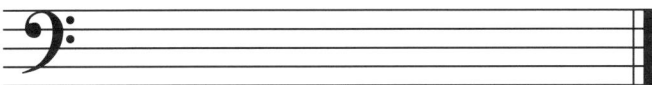

c) The following melody is in D minor, in 2/4 time.

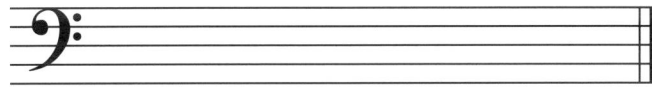

d) The following melody is in E minor, in 2/4 time.

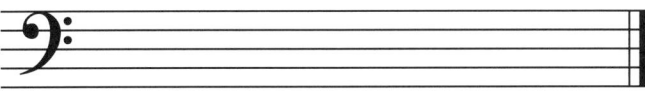

e) The following melody is in B minor, in 2/4 time.

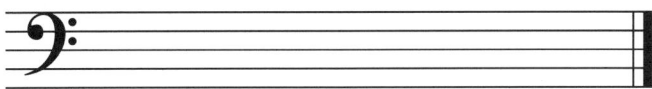

Check the appropriate box on p. 125.

Melody Master

Set Five

a) The following melody is in G major, in 4/4 time.

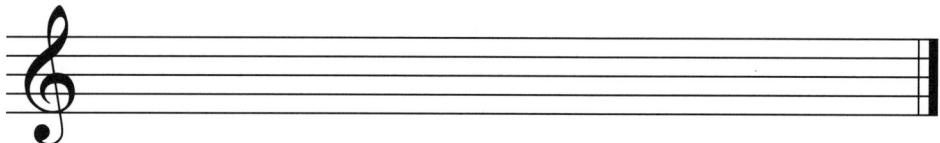

b) The following melody is in D minor, in 2/4 time..

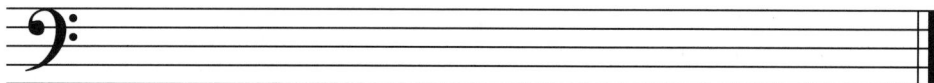

c) The following melody is in C major, in 3/4 time.

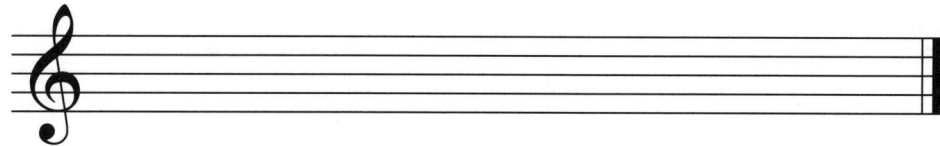

d) The following melody is in D major, in 3/4 time.

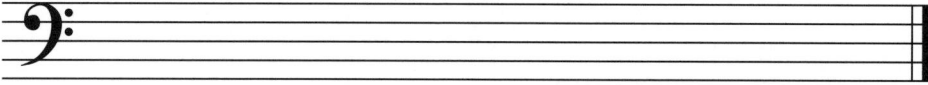

e) The following melody is in G minor, in 4/4 time.

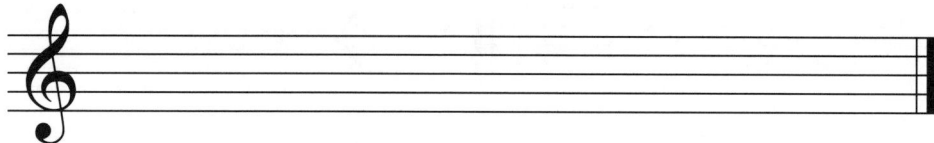

Check the appropriate box on p. 125.

Charts and Games

Rhythm Jumble Chart

Each time you learn a new rhythmic unit, circle it on the Rhythm Jumble Chart.

Use the Rhythm Jumble Chart to practice rhythms for *one minute* every day. Tap the beat with your finger as you point to the rhythmic unit you are singing. Sing each unit two or three times before moving on to the next one. Gradually start mixing them up by randomly pointing to different units. Try not to miss a beat!

You can also use this chart to play any of the Rhythm Jumble games described on the next page.

These units are all based on the quarter-note beat!

Charts and Games

Rhythm Jumble Games

Rhythm Jumble Reading

The goal of this sight-reading game is to sing all the circled rhythmic units on the Rhythm Jumble Chart in random order, while keeping a steady beat. To play Rhythm Jumble Reading, you will need someone to keep track of the number of units you can sing correctly without stopping. You win the game when you can successfully sing at least one more unit than the last time you played. Record your score in the Rhythm Jumble score boxes on your Theory Worksheets. When you can sing 32 units correctly, you will earn the official title of Rhythm Jumble "Reading Expert" and you may write the letters "RE" in the score box.

The rules are:

1) Tap a steady beat with your finger.
2) Point to each rhythmic unit as you sing it.
3) Sing a unit only twice before you move to a new one.
4) Sing the units in random order.
5) You are "out" if you sing a unit incorrectly or if your steady beat falters.

As you become more proficient, you can make the Rhythm Jumble Reading game more challenging by increasing the tempo. You can also change rule 3 so that you sing a unit only *once* before you move on to the next one. (Students in group classes can play this game in teams and adapt the rules to meet their needs.)

Rhythm Jumble Solitaire

The rules for Rhythm Jumble Solitaire are the same as for Rhythm Jumble Reading, except that you can play without a helper. All you need is a timer. Keep track of the number of seconds that you can continuously sing the rhythmic units in random order before you make a mistake or your steady beat falters. You win the game when you have increased your time from your previous score. Record your scores in the Rhythm Jumble score boxes on your Theory Worksheets. When you can sing random units continuously for one minute, you will have earned the official title of Rhythm Jumble "Solitaire Expert" and you may write the letters "SE" in the score boxes on your Theory Worksheets.

Rhythm Jumble Composer

To play Rhythm Jumble Composer, you need to make a set of rhythm cards. Use the rhythmic units on the Rhythm Jumble Chart (p. 129). Draw each rhythmic unit on a blank card. Make two copies of each unit. You should have a total of 32 cards.

Compose your own rhythmic pattern by laying out a series of cards from left to right in any order you choose. You can also shuffle the cards to mix them up before laying them out. Tap a steady beat while you point to each card in turn and sing your new rhythmic pattern. Keep track of how many cards you can sing correctly without faltering in your steady beat. Record your score in the boxes on the Theory Worksheets. When you can correctly sing a pattern that uses all 32 cards, you will earn the official title of Rhythm Jumble "Composing Expert" and you may write the letters "CE" in the score boxes on your Theory Worksheets.

Charts and Games

Terms and Symbols Chart

This chart lists definitions for all the terms and symbols covered in this volume.

Expression Marks

Italian Term	Symbol	Definition
crescendo or *cresc.*	&lt;	gradually getting louder
decrescendo or *decresc.*	&gt;	gradually getting softer
diminuendo or *dim.*	&gt;	gradually getting softer

Dynamic Markings

Italian Term	Symbol	Definition
pianissimo	*pp*	very soft
piano	*p*	soft
mezzo piano	*mp*	medium soft
mezzo forte	*mf*	medium loud
forte	*f*	loud
fortissimo	*ff*	very loud

Tempo

Italian Term	Definition
largo	slow and stately
adagio	slow; between *largo* and *andante*
andante	a walking pace; medium speed
moderato	a moderate speed; faster than *andante*
allegretto	fairly fast but slower than *allegro*
allegro	fast and lively
presto	faster than *allegro*

Charts and Games

Miscellaneous Terms and Symbols

Term	Sign	Definition
staccato		short and detached
legato		smooth and connected
slur		play the notes *legato*
tie		hold for combined value of the tied notes
accent		emphasize or stress
fermata	𝄐	hold the note longer than the written value
da capo al fine	D.C. al Fine	go back to the beginning and play until the *Fine* (end)
metronome marking	M.M.	a mechanical device that ticks a set number of times each minute so you can determine the tempo
repeat sign		repeat from the beginning
repeat signs		repeat the material within the repeat signs

Charts and Games

Song Clue Chart

This chart shows ascending and descending intervals and provides several song clue examples for each one. There is also space for you to add your own song clues. Each time you learn a new interval, you will be instructed to turn to this chart to put a check beside the interval.

Ascending Intervals ↗	✔	Possible Song Clues	Your Own Clues
min 2		Oh, Danny Boy Theme from *The Pink Panther* The Entertainer	
maj 2		Are You Sleeping? Yankee Doodle "Do, a Deer" from *The Sound of Music*	
min 3		Brahms' Lullaby O Canada Greensleeves/What Child Is This?	
maj 3		Oh, When the Saints Go Marching In For He's a Jolly Good Fellow Theme from *Harry Potter*	
P4		Bridal Song ("Here Comes the Bride") We Wish You a Merry Christmas Theme from *Hockey Night in Canada*	
P5		Twinkle, Twinkle, Little Star Lavender's Blue Theme from *Star Wars*	
maj 6		My Bonnie Lies over the Ocean "Colors of the Wind" from *Pocahontas* Jingle Bells ("Dashing through the snow…")	
maj 7		"Bali Ha'i" from *South Pacific*	
P8		Sing a Song of Sixpence Somewhere, over the Rainbow Let It Snow ("Oh, the weather outside…")	

Sound Advice Level 4

Charts and Games

Descending Intervals ↘	✔	Possible Song Clues	Your Own Clues
min 2		Joy to the World Jingle Bell Rock Für Elise	
maj 2		Three Blind Mice Mary Had a Little Lamb Deck the Halls	
min 3		Star Spangled Banner Rain, Rain, Go Away Ring Around the Rosie	
maj 3		Opening motive from Beethoven's 5th Symphony Good Night, Ladies Swing Low, Sweet Chariot Westminster Chimes	
P4		*Eine kleine Nachtmusik* Oh Come, All Ye Faithful Organ music played at hockey games!	
P5		Minuet in G Major by Petzold Theme from *The Flinstones*	
min 6		Theme from *Love Story* Please Don't Talk About Me When I'm Gone	
P8		Hot Cross Buns Jump, Jive, and Wail There's No Business Like Show Business	

Charts and Games

Mad Music Games

There are three Mad Music Games in Level 4.

1) The major key signature naming game begins in Lesson 3. The goal is to accurately name all the major keys on the chart in twenty seconds or less.

2) The interval naming game—Name the 3rds—begins in Lesson 8. The goal is to accurately name all the major and minor 3rds on the chart in two minutes or less.

3) The minor key signature game begins in Lesson 13. The goal is to accurately name all the minor keys on the chart in twenty seconds or less.

When you achieve the goals in all three games, you will have earned the status of "Mad Music Expert" and will be awarded a Certificate of Achievement (see the inside back cover). We suggest you continue to play all three Mad Music Games at least once a week even after you achieve Expert status. For a more challenging key signature game, name both the major keys and the minor keys for each key signature on the charts.

The easiest way to play Mad Music is to have someone follow the answer sheet while you give the answers out loud.

Beginning with Lesson 3, you will often be asked to record three Mad Music scores on your Theory Worksheets. This means that part of your homework assignment for that lesson is to play Mad Music at least three times. If you can complete the more challenging key signature game (combining major and minor keys), write "Challenge Level" (CE) in the box where you record your score.

Charts and Games

Mad Music

Major and Minor Key Signatures

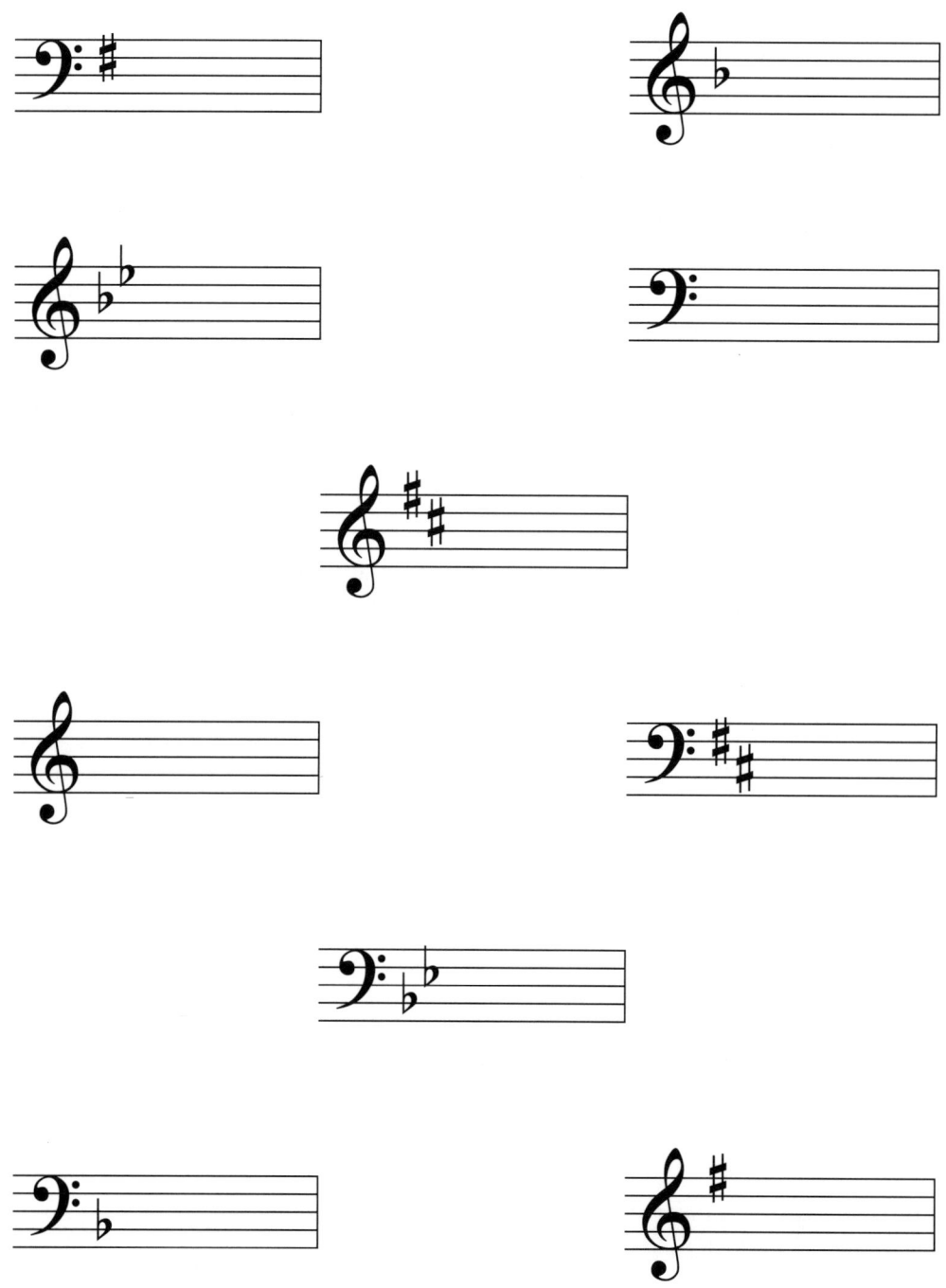

Charts and Games

Mad Music

Name the 3rds (Major or Minor)

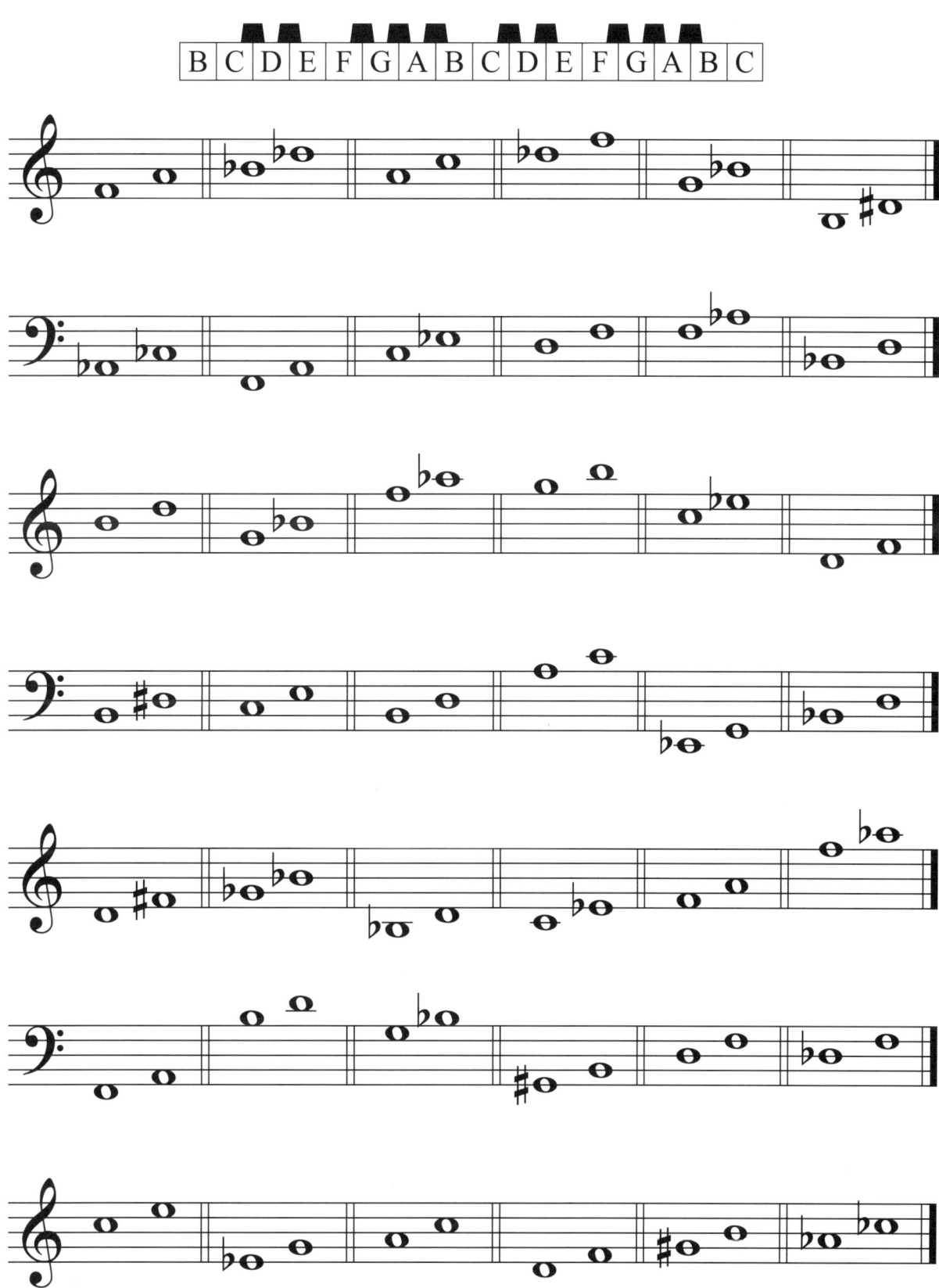

Sound Advice Level 4

Answer Keys

Lesson 1

1 Rhythmic Reading:

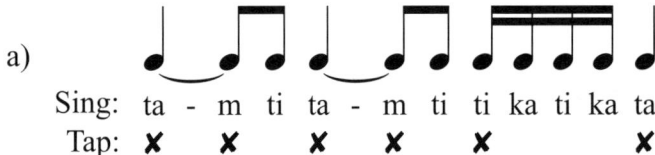

2 Rhythmic Reading:

3 Rhythm Singback/Clapback:

4 Rhythm Singback/Clapback:

5 Rhythmic Identification:

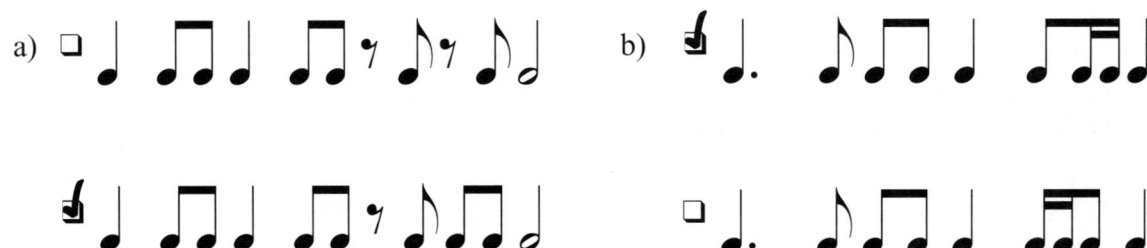

Ear-Training Answer Key

Lesson 2

 1 Editing:

 2 Rhythmic Identification:

 3 Rhythm Singback/Clapback:

 4 Sight Singing:

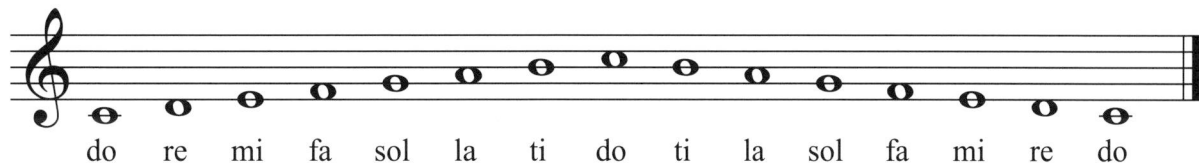

do re mi fa sol la ti do ti la sol fa mi re do

 5 Sight Singing:

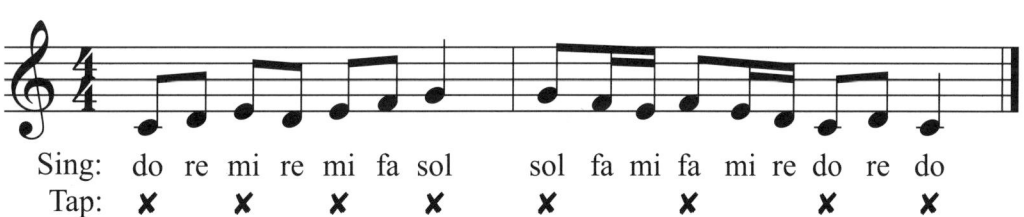

Sing: do re mi re mi fa sol sol fa mi fa mi re do re do
Tap: ✗ ✗ ✗ ✗ ✗ ✗ ✗ ✗

Ear-Training Answer Key

Lesson 3

 1 Rhythmic Identification:

a)    b)

 2 Rhythm Singback/Clapback:

 3 Sight Singing:

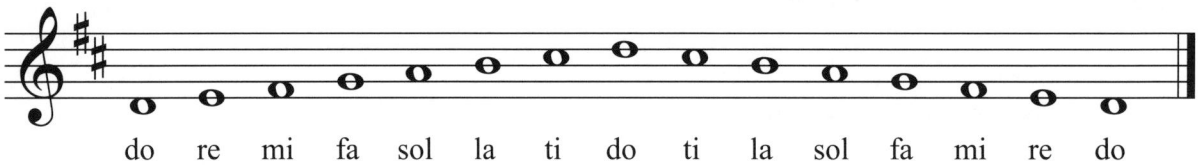

do re mi fa sol la ti do ti la sol fa mi re do

 4 Sight Singing:

D major

Sing: do re mi fa sol fa mi re mi fa sol la sol la sol fa mi re do____
Tap: ✗   ✗   ✗   ✗   ✗   ✗   ✗   ✗

 5 Melody Singback/Playback:

Ear-Training Answer Key

Lesson 4

 1 Sight Singing:

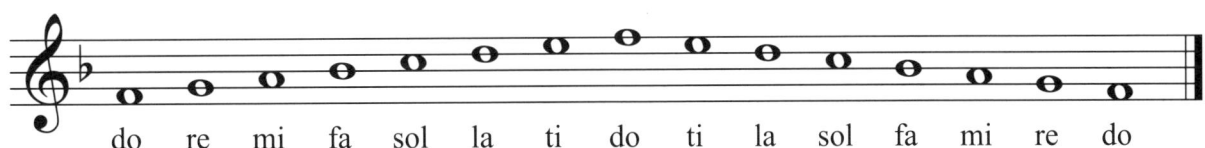

do re mi fa sol la ti do ti la sol fa mi re do

 2 Sight Singing:

F major

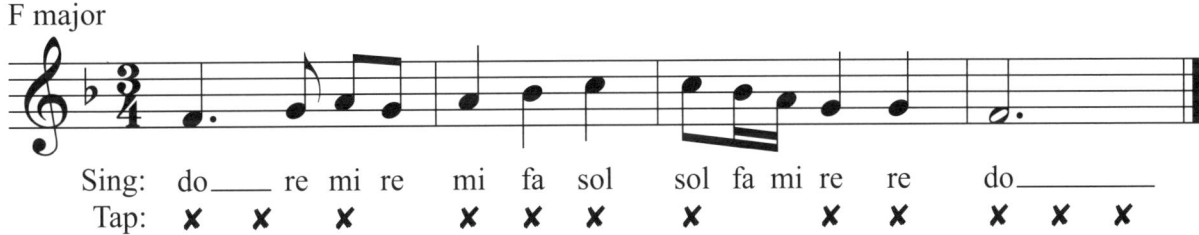

Sing: do___ re mi re mi fa sol sol fa mi re re do___
Tap: x x x x x x x x x x x x x

 3 Rhythmic Reading:

Sing: ti ti ti ka ti ka ti ti ka ta ka ti ka ka ti ka ti ti ta
Tap: x x x x x x x x x

 4 Rhythm Singback/Clapback:

 5 Rhythmic Dictation:

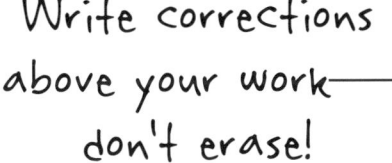

Write corrections above your work— don't erase!

6 Meter Identification:

a) ☐ duple b) ☑ duple
   ☑ triple   ☐ triple

Sound Advice Level 4   Ear-Training Answer Key   141

Ear-Training Answer Key

Lesson 5

 1 **Sight Singing:**

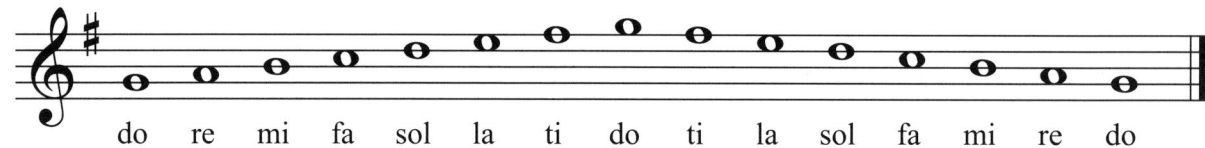

 2 **Sight Singing:**

 3 **Interval Identification:**

    a) maj 2   b) P5   c) maj 3   d) P8   e) maj 6

    f) P4   g) maj 7   h) maj 3   i) P4   j) maj 6

 4 **Rhythm Clapback:**

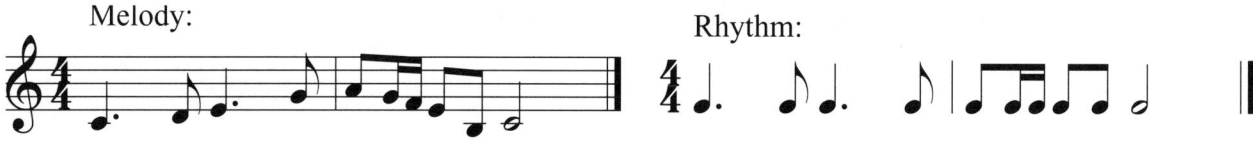

5 **Melody Singback/Playback:**

Ear-Training Answer Key

Lesson 6

 1 Sight Singing:

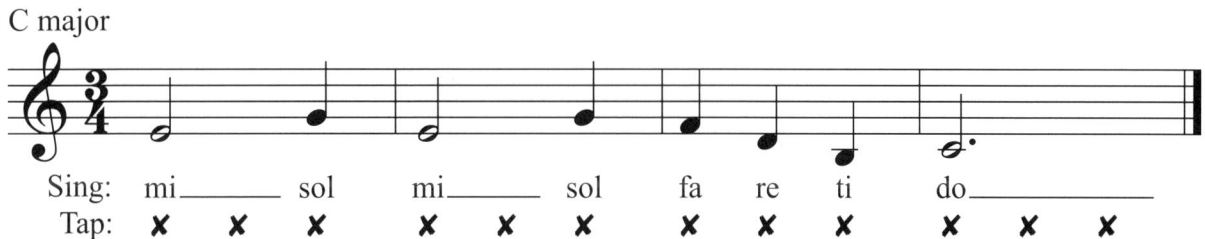

 2 Interval Identification:

a) min 2   b) min 3   c) maj 2   d) maj 3   e) maj 2   f) min 2   g) min 3

 3 Editing:

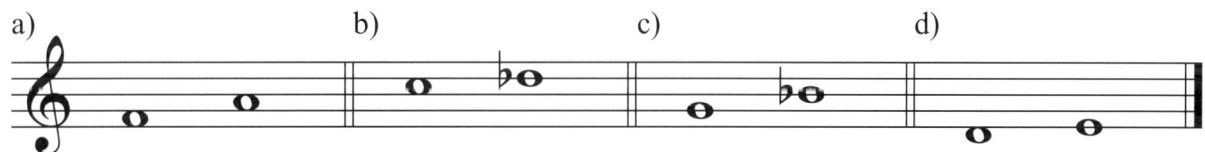

 4 Melodic Dictation:

 5 Rhythmic Dictation:

Ear-Training Answer Key

Lesson 7

1 **Interval Identification:**

a) maj 7   b) min 3   c) P4   d) min 2   e) P5

f) maj 6   g) maj 2   h) P8   i) min 2   j) maj 6

2 **Sight Singing:**

3 **Editing:**

4 **Rhythm Clapback:**

5 **Melodic Dictation:**

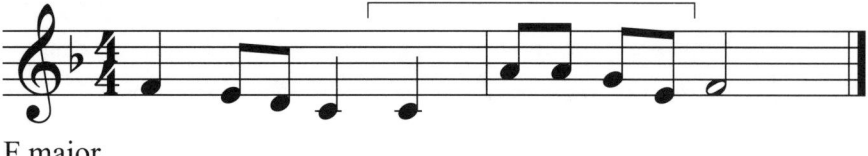

F major

6 **Melodic Improvisation:**

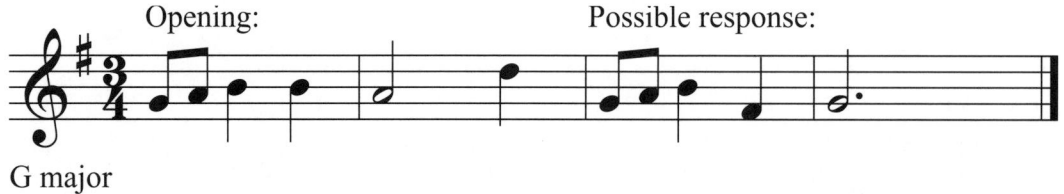

G major

Ear-Training Answer Key

Lesson 8

 1 **Sight Singing:**

 2 **Interval Identification:**

    a) P8   b) maj 3   c) min 2   d) maj 7   e) P5

    f) min 3   g) maj 6   h) P4   i) min 2   j) maj 2

 3 **Editing:**

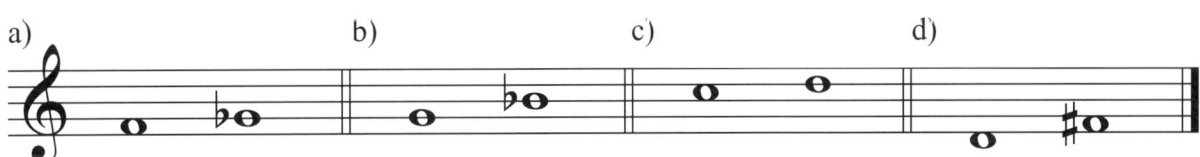

 4 **Melodic Dictation:**

 5 **Rhythmic Dictation:**

Ear-Training Answer Key

Lesson 9

1 **Interval Identification:**

a) ↘ P5 b) ↘ min 3 c) ↘ P8 d) ↘ min 3 e) ↘ P5

f) ↗ maj 3 g) ↗ P4 h) ↗ maj 6 i) ↗ min 2 j) ↗ P5

2 **Triad Identification:**

a) maj b) min c) min d) maj e) min

3 **Editing:**

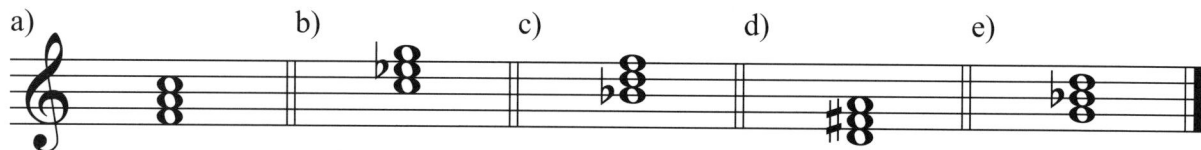

4 **Triads:**

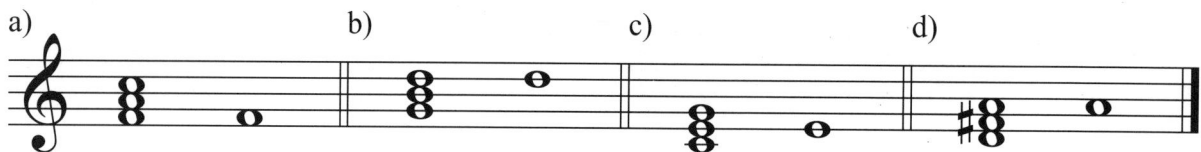

5 **Sight Singing:**

Ear-Training Answer Key

Lesson 10

 1 **Interval Identification:**

a) ↘ min 3   b) ↘ P8   c) ↘ P5   d) ↘ min 3   e) ↘ P8

f) ↗ maj 2   g) ↗ P8   h) ↗ min 3   i) ↗ P4   j) ↗ maj 3

 2 **Sight Singing:**

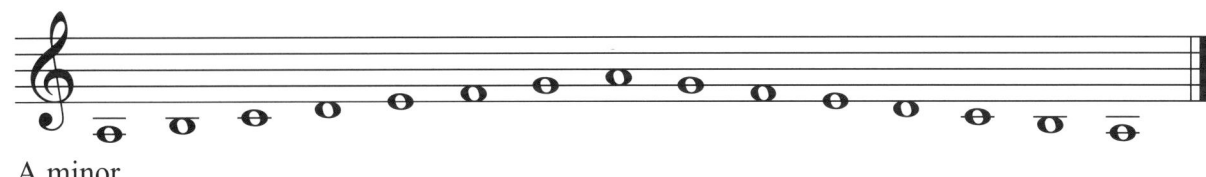

A minor

 3 **Sight Singing:**

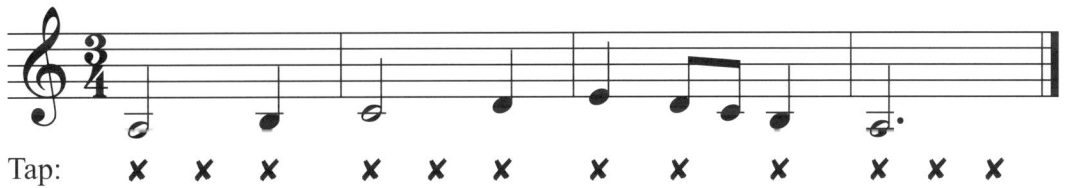

Tap:

 4 **Scale Identification:**

a) maj   b) nm   c) nm   d) maj

 5 **Triads:**

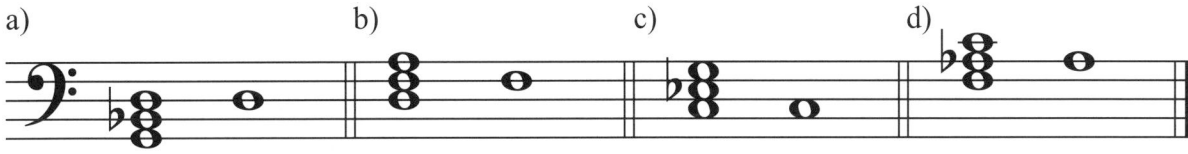

 6 **Melodic Improvisation:**

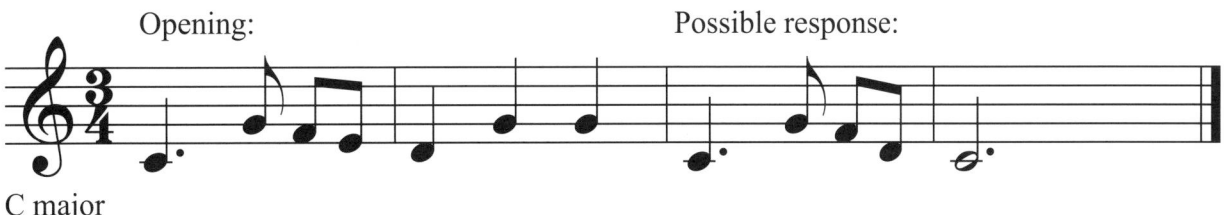

C major

Ear-Training Answer Key

Lesson 11

 1 **Interval Identification:**

a) ↘ P5   b) ↘ min 3   c) ↘ P8   d) ↘ min 3   e) ↘ P8

f) ↗ maj 3   g) ↗ P5   h) ↗ min 2   i) ↗ maj 6   j) ↗ P8

 2 **Scale Identification:**

a) maj   b) min   c) min   d) maj   e) min

 3 **Sight Singing:**

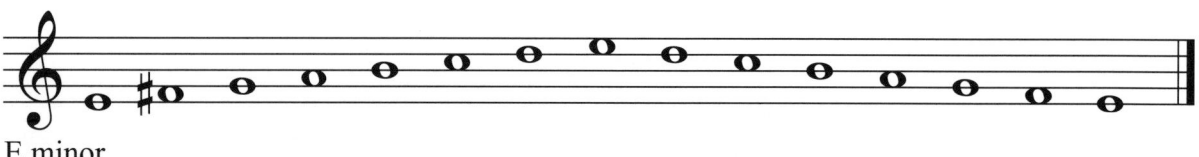

E minor

 4 **Sight Singing:**

Ma-jor league to mi-nor league, woe is me! Half step, whole step, mi-nor key!

 5 **Sight Singing:**

Mi-nor league to ma-jor league, good for me! Whole step, half step ma-jor key!

Ear-Training Answer Key

Lesson 12

1 Interval Identification:

a) ↗ maj 3   b) ↗ P8   c) ↘ min 3   d) ↗ maj 6   e) ↗ min 3

f) ↘ P5   g) ↗ maj 2   h) ↗ P4   i) ↘ P8   j) ↗ maj 7

2 Scale Identification:

a) min   b) maj   c) min   d) min   e) maj

3 Sight Singing:

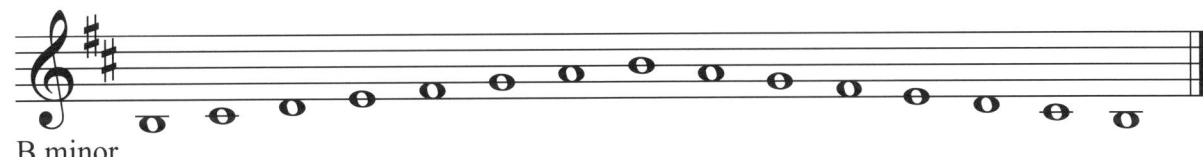
B minor

4 Rhythmic Reading:

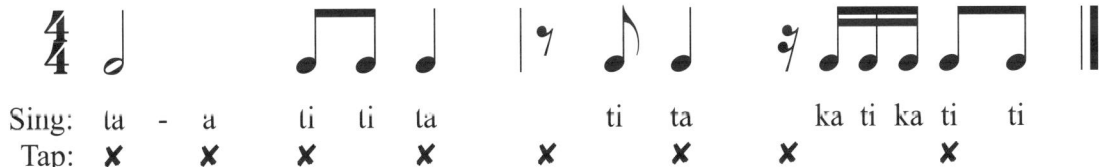

Sing: ta - a   ti ti ta   ti ta   ka ti ka ti ti
Tap: ✗   ✗   ✗ ✗ ✗   ✗ ✗   ✗

5 Rhythmic Identification:

a)    b)

6 Melody Singback/Playback:

B minor

Ear-Training Answer Key

Lesson 13

1 **Interval Identification:**

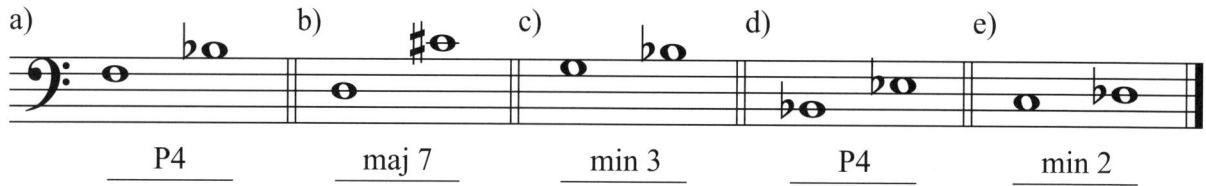

2 **Rhythmic Dictation:**

3 **Melodic Dictation:**

G minor

4 **Melodic Improvisation:**

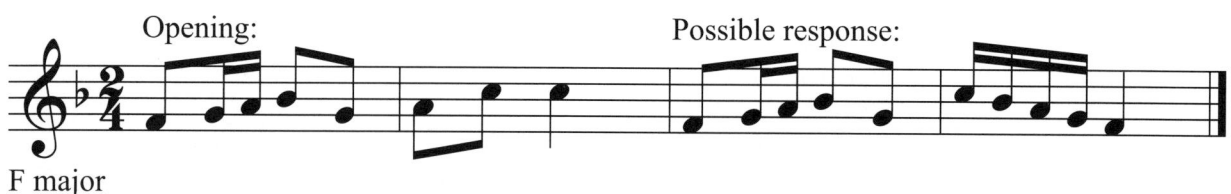

F major

5 **Editing:**

Ear-Training Answer Key

Lesson 14

1 Interval Identification:

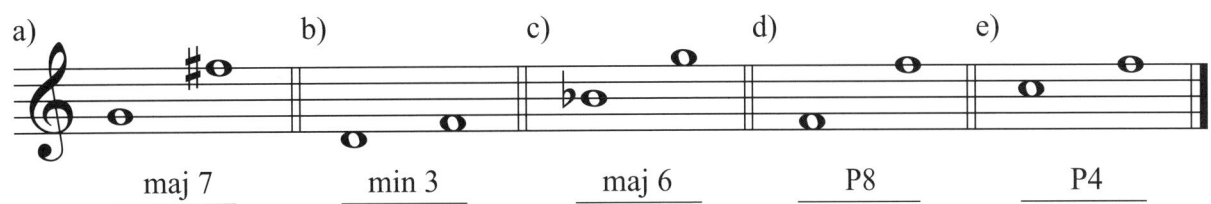

a) maj 7   b) min 3   c) maj 6   d) P8   e) P4

2 Rhythmic Reading:

Sing: tim ka tim ka ti ti ta ti ka ti ka ti tim ka ta
Tap: ✗ ✗ ✗ ✗ ✗ ✗ ✗ ✗

3 Rhythmic Dictation:

4 Triad Identification:

a) maj   b) maj   c) min   d) min   e) maj

5 Triads:

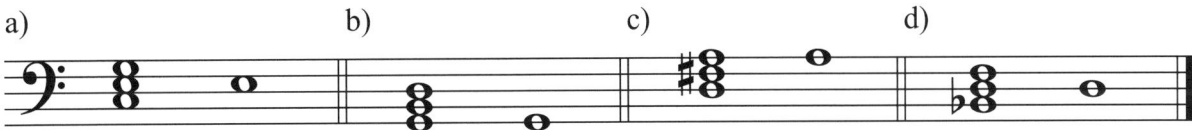

6 Melodic Improvisation:

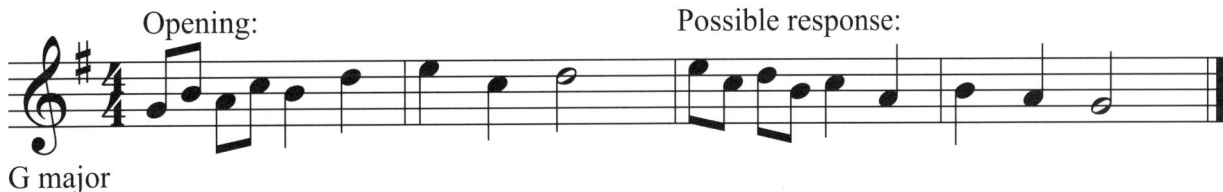

Opening: Possible response:

G major

Ear-Training Answer Key

Lesson 15

1 **Interval Identification:**

    a) ↘ maj 3   b) ↘ P8   c) ↘ P4   d) ↘ maj 3   e) ↘ P5

    f) ↗ maj 3   g) ↗ min 2   h) ↗ maj 6   i) ↗ P5   j) ↗ maj 2

2 **Sight Singing:**

3 **Rhythm Clapback:**

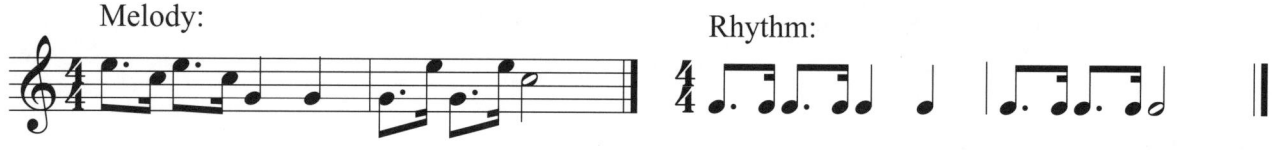

4 **Melodic Dictation:**

5 **Melodic Improvisation:**

Ear-Training Answer Key

Lesson 16

 1 **Interval Identification:**

a) ↗ P8   b) ↘ min 3   c) ↗ maj 6   d) ↘ P5   e) ↗ P4

f) ↘ maj 3   g) ↗ maj 3   h) ↘ P4   i) ↗ min 2   j) ↗ maj 2

 2 **Sight Singing:**

 3 **Editing:**

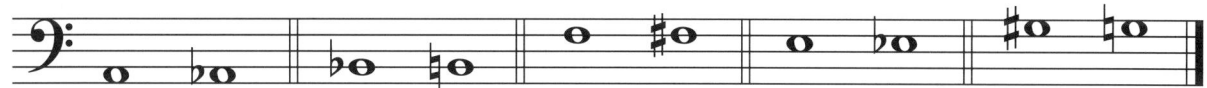

 4 **Rhythmic Dictation:**

Melody: Rhythm:

 5 **Melodic Dictation:**

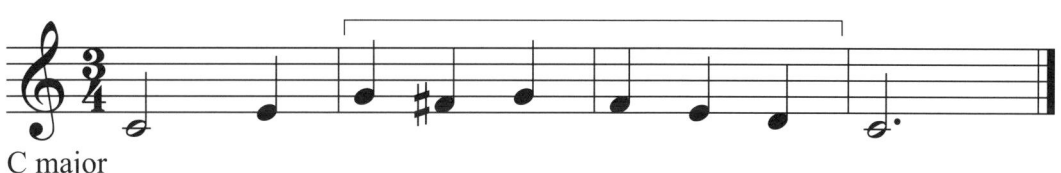

C major

 6 **Melodic Improvisation:**

Opening: Possible response:

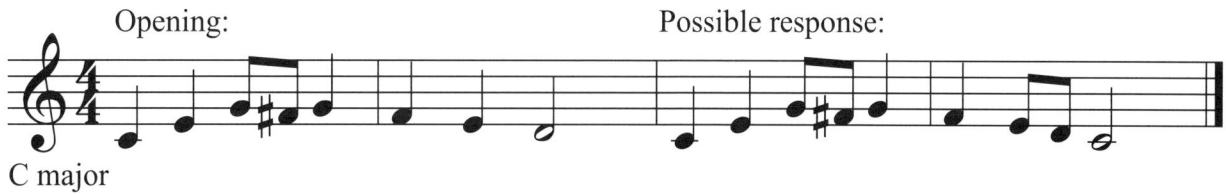

C major

Ear-Training Answer Key

Lesson 17

 1 **Interval Identification:**

a) ↗ min 2   b) ↘ P4   c) ↗ min 3   d) ↘ min 3   e) ↗ P4

f) ↘ maj 3   g) ↗ maj 7   h) ↘ P8   i) ↗ maj 6   j) ↘ P5

 2 **Sight Singing:**

D minor

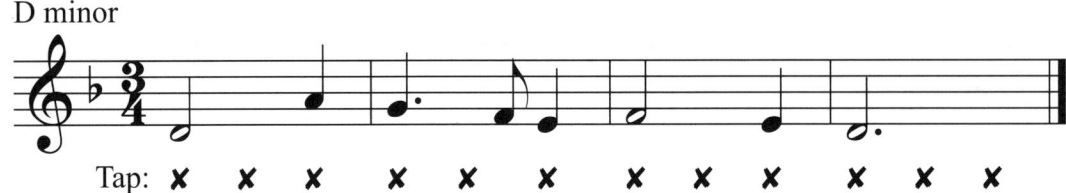

 3 **Rhythmic Dictation:**

Melody: Rhythm:

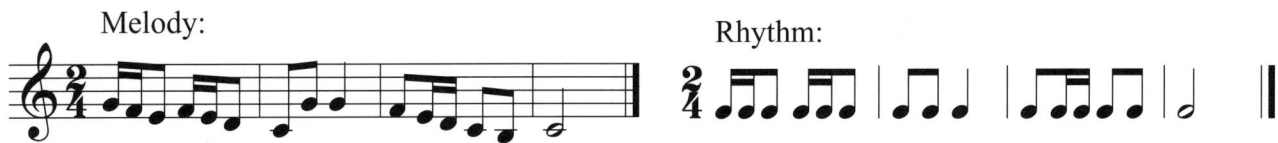

 4 **Melodic Dictation:**

G minor

 5 **Melodic Improvisation:**

Opening: Possible response:

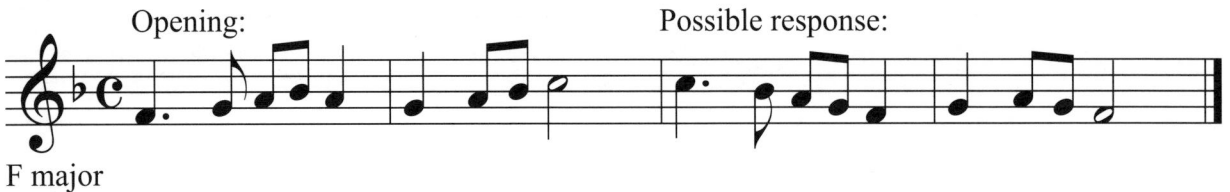

F major

Ear-Training Answer Key

Lesson 18

 1 Interval Identification:

a) ↘ min 2 b) ↗ P4 c) ↗ min 3 d) ↘ maj 2 e) ↗ P5

f) ↗ maj 6 g) ↘ min 2 h) ↗ maj 7 i) ↗ maj 3 j) ↘ maj 2

 2 Sight Singing:

C major

 3 Rhythmic Reading:

Sing: ti ti ti ti ti ti ta ti tum
Tap: ✗   ✗   ✗   ✗

 4 Rhythm Singback/Clapback:

 5 Rhythm Singback/Clapback:

 6 Rhythmic Identification:

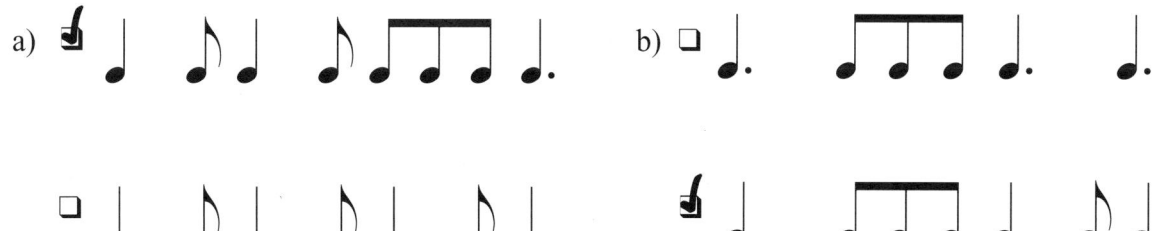

Sound Advice Level 4   Ear-Training Answer Key   155

Ear-Training Answer Key

Lesson 19

 1 **Interval Identification:**

a) ↗ maj 7   b) ↗ maj 2   c) ↗ P8   d) ↘ P4   e) ↗ P5

f) ↘ min 2   g) ↗ maj 3   h) ↘ P8   i) ↘ maj 3   j) ↗ min 2

 2 **Melody Singback/Playback:**

D minor

 3 **Rhythmic Reading:**

Sing: ta   ti ti ti ti ta   ti tum
Tap: ✗   ✗   ✗   ✗

 4 **Rhythm Singback/Clapback:**

 5 **Rhythmic Identification:**

a)    b)

 6 **Editing:**

G major

Ear-Training Answer Key

Lesson 20

1 **Interval Identification:**

a) ↘ min 6   b) ↗ maj 2   c) ↗ maj 7   d) ↘ maj 3   e) ↘ min 6

f) ↗ P8   g) ↘ P4   h) ↗ min 2   i) ↘ min 6   j) ↗ P4

2 **Sight Singing:**

A minor

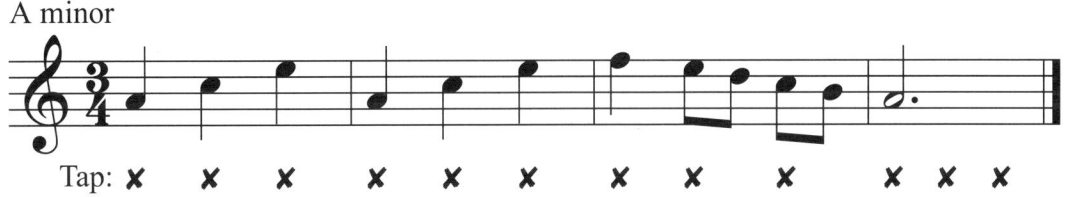

3 **Triads:**

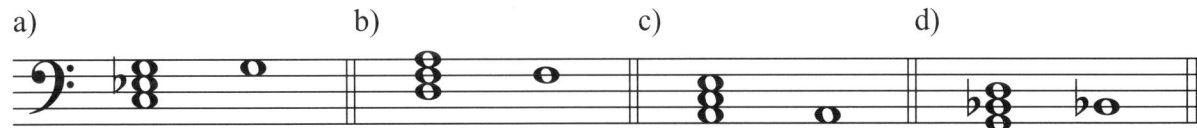

4 **Rhythmic Reading:**

5 **Error Detection:**

6 **Melodic Improvisation:**

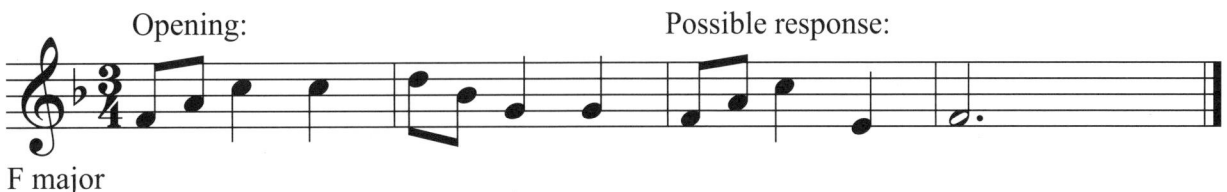

F major

Ear-Training Answer Key

Lesson 21

1. Interval Identification:

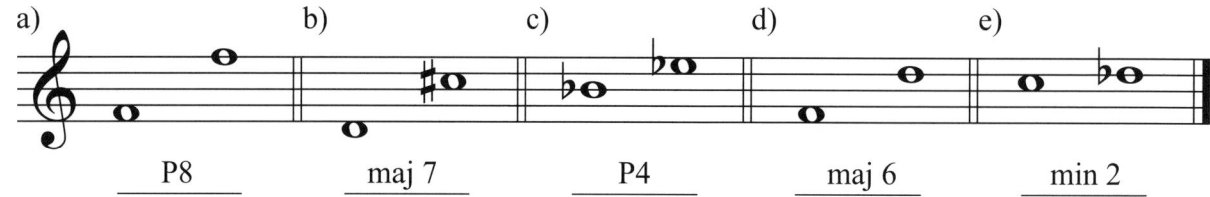

P8, maj 7, P4, maj 6, min 2

2. Melody Singback/Playback:

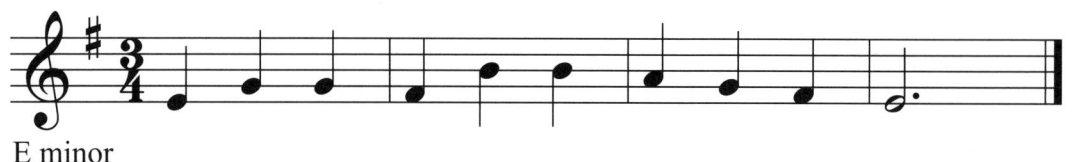

E minor

3. Rhythmic Dictation:

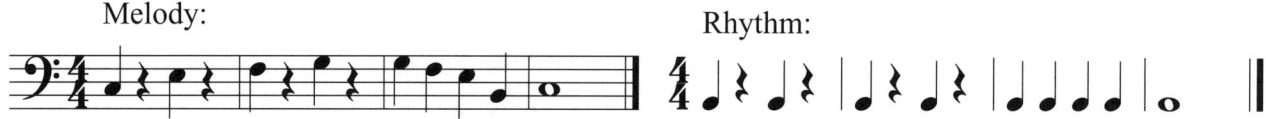

4. Error Detection:

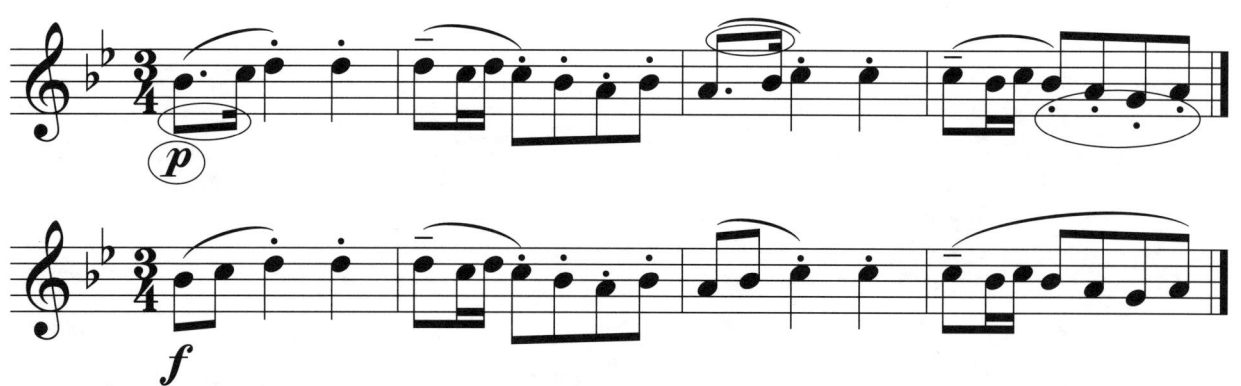

5. Texture Identification:

a) ☐ polyphonic   b) ☑ polyphonic
   ☑ homophonic   ☐ homophonic

Ear-Training Answer Key

Lesson 22

1 **Interval Identification:**

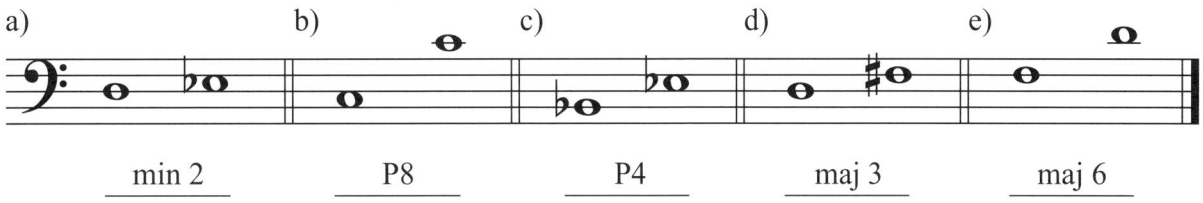

2 **Melodic Improvisation:**

3 **Rhythmic Dictation:**

4 **Error Detection:**

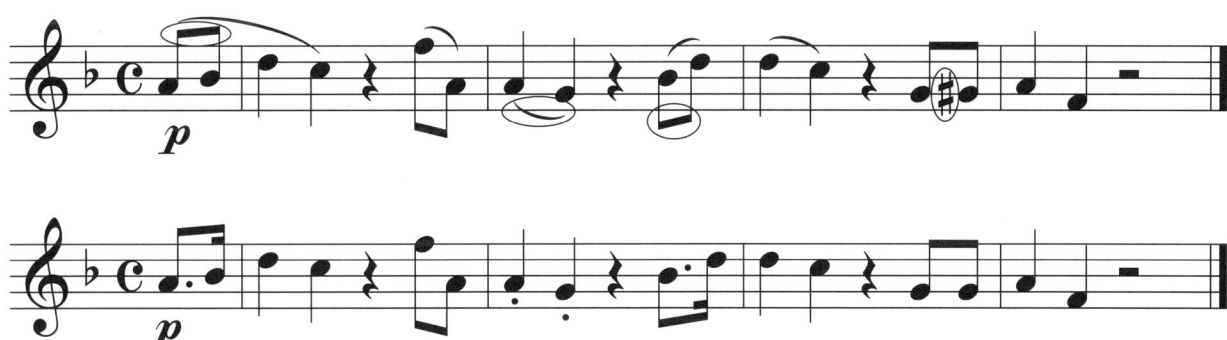

5 **Texture Identification:**

a) ☐ polyphonic
✓ homophonic

b) ✓ polyphonic
☐ homophonic

Ear-Training Answer Key

Lesson 23

1 **Interval Identification:**

    a) ↘ min 6   b) ↗ P4   c) ↗ maj 6   d) ↘ maj 3   e) ↗ maj 7

    f) ↗ maj 2   g) ↘ P4   h) ↗ min 3   i) ↘ min 2   j) ↗ P5

2 **Melody Singback/Playback:**

D minor

3 **Melodic Dictation:**

F major

4 **Triads:**

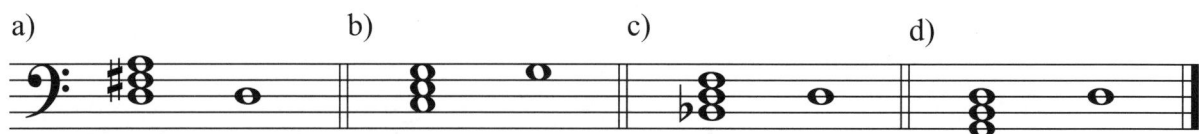

5 **Texture Identification:**

    a) ☑ polyphonic   b) ☐ polyphonic
       ☐ homophonic   ☑ homophonic

Ear-Training Answer Key

Lesson 24

1 **Interval Identification:**

a) ↗ min 2   b) ↘ P4   c) ↘ maj 2   d) ↗ min 3   e) ↘ min 6

f) ↘ min 2   g) ↗ maj 3   h) ↘ P8   i) ↗ P5   j) ↘ maj 3

2 **Triads:**

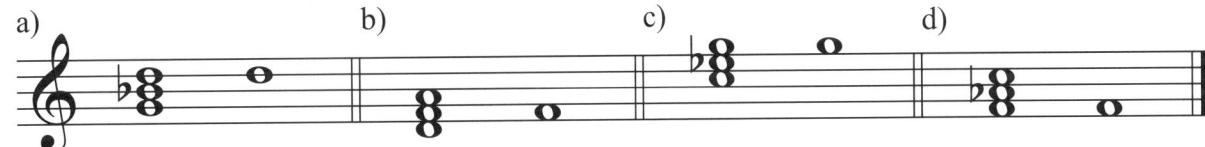

3 **Melody Singback/Playback:**

B minor

4 **Melodic Dictation:**

D major

5 **Error Detection:**

Melody Master Answer Key

Set One

a) The following melody is in C major, in 4/4 time.

b) The following melody is in F major, in 3/4 time.

c) The following melody is in G major, in 2/4 time.

d) The following melody is in D major, in 4/4 time.

e) The following melody is in B♭ major, in 3/4 time.

Check the appropriate box on p. 125.

Set Two

a) The following melody is in C major, in 3/4 time.

b) The following melody is in D major, in 3/4 time.

c) The following melody is in F major, in 4/4 time.

d) The following melody is in G major, in 3/4 time.

e) The following melody is in B♭ major, in 4/4 time.

Check the appropriate box on p. 125.

Melody Master Answer Key

Set Three

a) The following melody is in A minor, in 3/4 time.

b) The following melody is in D minor, in 4/4 time.

c) The following melody is in E minor, in 4/4 time.

d) The following melody is in G minor, in 3/4 time.

e) The following melody is in A minor, in 4/4 time.

Check the appropriate box on p. 125.

Set Four

a) The following melody is in A minor, in 2/4 time.

b) The following melody is in G minor, in 2/4 time.

c) The following melody is in D minor, in 2/4 time.

d) The following melody is in E minor, in 2/4 time.

e) The following melody is in B minor, in 2/4 time.

Check the appropriate box on p. 125.

Sound Advice Level 4   Melody Master Answer Key

Melody Master Answer Key

Set Five

a) The following melody is in G major, in 4/4 time.

b) The following melody is in D minor, in 2/4 time.

c) The following melody is in C major, in 3/4 time.

d) The following melody is in D major, in 3/4 time.

e) The following melody is in G minor, in 4/4 time.

Check the appropriate box on p. 125.

Mad Music Answer Key

Major and Minor Key Signatures

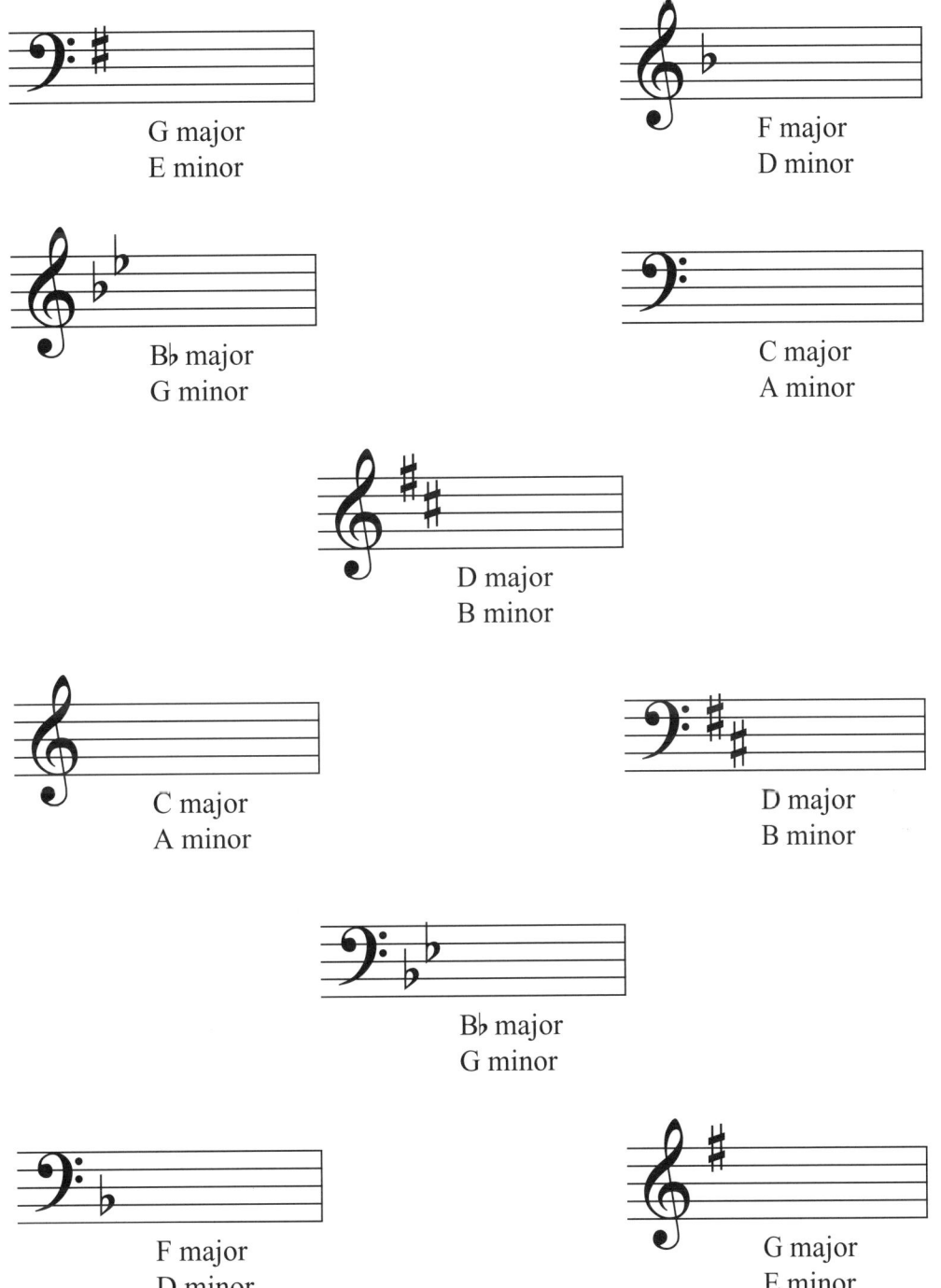

Mad Music Answer Key

Name the 3rds (Major or Minor)

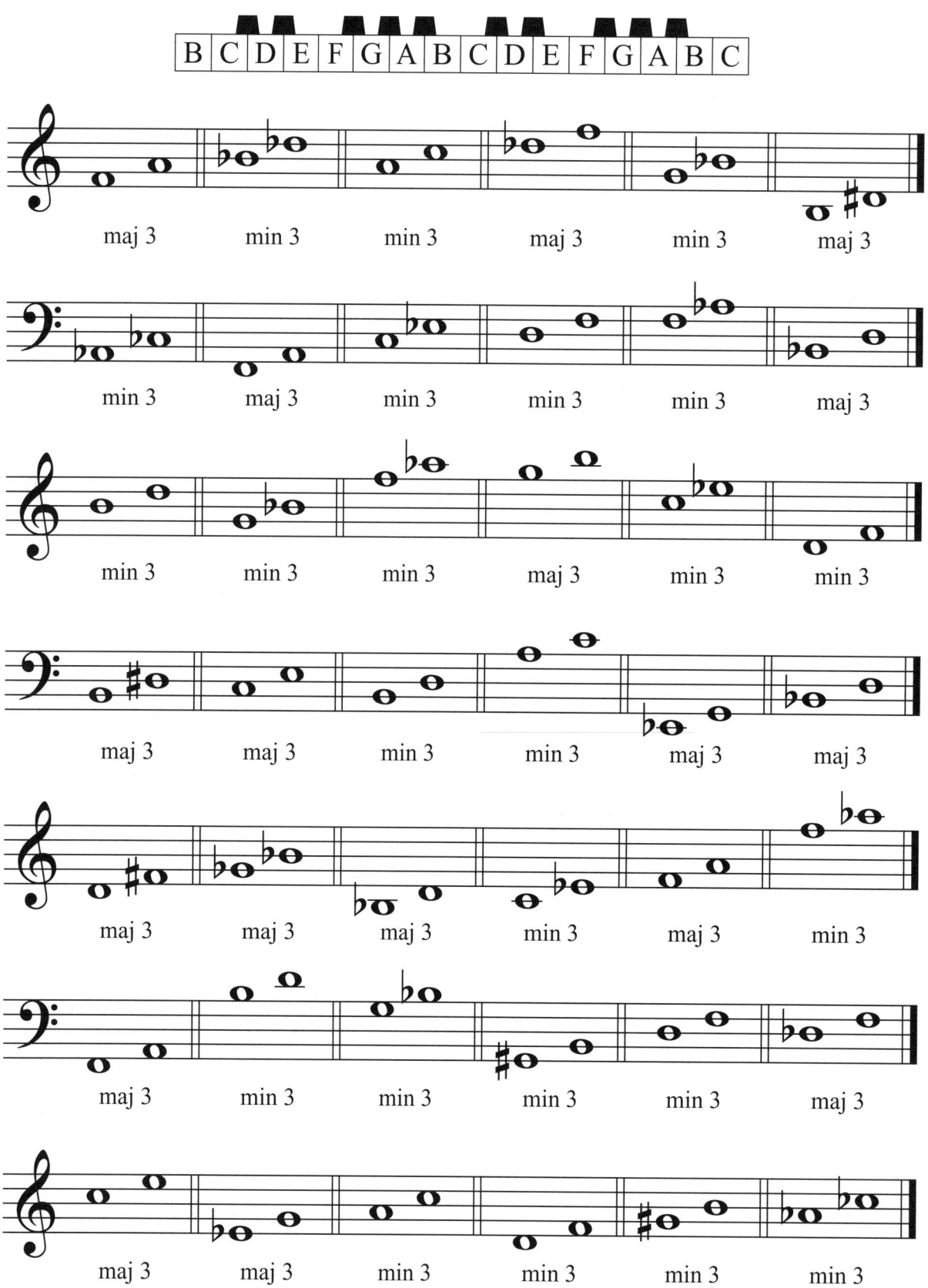

Appendix

Sight-Singing Syllable Systems

Movable Do

In the *movable do* system, do represents the tonic or first degree of the scale, regardless of key. Accidentals are accounted for by changing the syllables.

The syllables for the movable do system are:

Major Scale

Natural Minor Scale

Harmonic Minor Scale

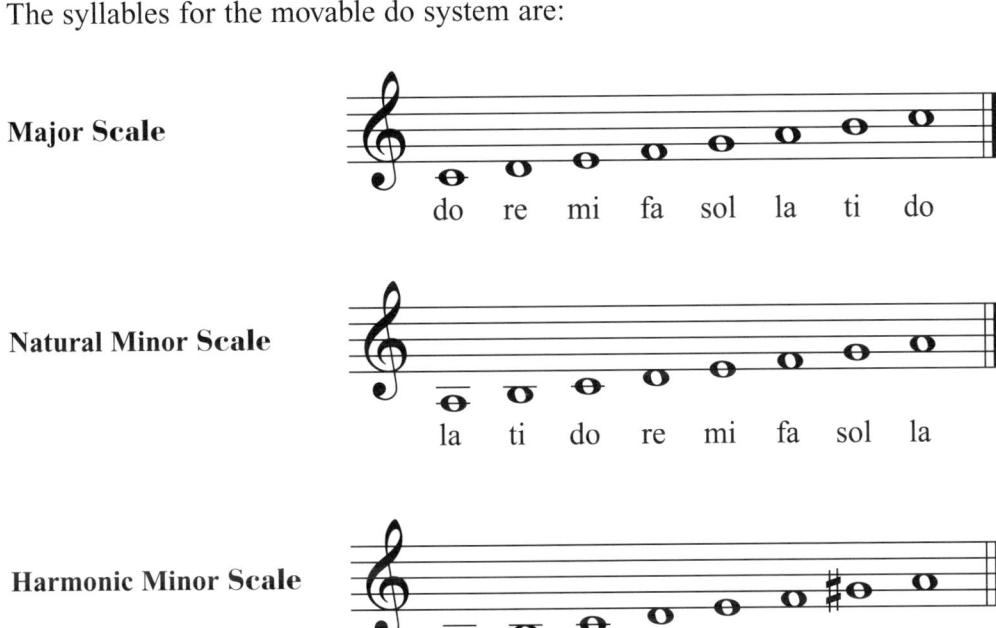

Melodic Minor Scale

Chromatic Scale

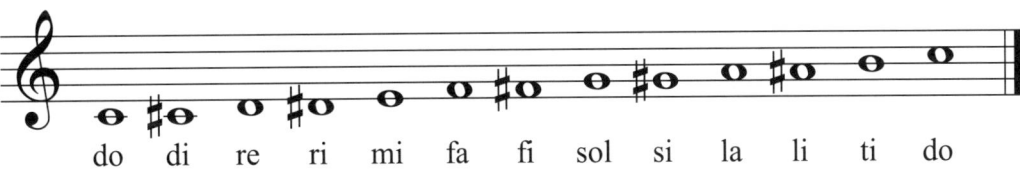

Appendix

Movable Do (continued)

Alternative syllables for minor scales are:

Natural Minor Scale: do re mé fa sol lé té do

Harmonic Minor Scale: do re mé fa sol lé ti do

Melodic Minor Scale: do re mé fa sol la ti do té lé sol fa mé re do

Numbers

In this system, numbers ($\hat{1}$, $\hat{2}$, $\hat{3}$, etc.) are used instead of syllables (do, re, mi, etc.). A carat (^) above a number identifies that number as a scale degree. The tonic or first degree of the scale is always $\hat{1}$, regardless of key. There is no numerical change for chromatic notes on the same degree of the scale.

Fixed Do

In the *fixed do* system, the syllables coincide with letter names of the notes, regardless of key. For example, C is always do, F is always fa, and so on. The syllables used in the fixed do system are the same as those shown above for the chromatic scale.